THE INTERNATIONAL COURT OF JUSTICE: 75 YEARS IN THE SERVICE OF PEACE AND JUSTICE

THE INTERNATIONAL COURT OF JUSTICE: 75 YEARS IN THE SERVICE OF PEACE AND JUSTICE

International Court of Justice
Cour internationale de Justice

A publication of the Registry of the International Court of Justice, The Hague, the Netherlands.

www.icj-cij.org

ISBN 978-92-1-003864-5

Sales number: 1203

TABLE OF CONTENTS

ARS
SCIENTIA

PREFACE

This publication, "The International Court of Justice: 75 years in the service of peace and justice", has been produced to mark the seventy-fifth anniversary of the inaugural sitting of the ICJ, held on 18 April 1946 at the Peace Palace in The Hague. It follows on from the illustrated book that was published in 2006 to celebrate the ICJ's sixtieth anniversary and re-released a decade later, in 2016, on the occasion of the seventieth anniversary of the "World Court".

This new book, produced entirely by the Registry, has been designed specifically with the general public in mind. It uses clear and accessible language to describe the Court and its activities, with the aim of fostering a better understanding of the ICJ's role and work and providing answers to the most frequently asked questions about the Court.

Readers will find information on how the Court functions, with each short chapter covering a different facet of the institution, including its human face. They will learn about the history of the Court, its judges and its Registry, the actors who may participate in proceedings before it, the principles governing its judicial activity and the contribution made by the Court to certain areas of international law.

In publishing this book, the Registry wishes not only to make the Court more accessible to the general public by shedding fresh light on its work, but also to celebrate what the institution has accomplished since its creation and pay tribute to all those who have contributed to its success over the past 75 years.

Philippe Gautier
Registrar

INTERN ALEDEJUSTICE
ERNATIONAL CO OF JUSTICE

INTRODUCTION: THE ICJ, 75 YEARS IN RETROSPECT

On 18 April 1946, the International Court of Justice (ICJ) held its opening session during a solemn inaugural sitting at the Peace Palace in The Hague. As the principal judicial organ of the United Nations, the Court was part of the international institutional framework devised in the aftermath of World War II. Its establishment was accompanied by formidable aspirations. It was hoped that the Court would contribute to "substituting orderly judicial processes for the vicissitudes of war and the reign of brutal force" (United Nations Conference on International Organization, 1945).

The Court's seventy-fifth anniversary, marked by the present publication, provides an opportunity to take stock of its accomplishments to date, in light of the founders' ambitious goals. Undoubtedly, the international community has changed significantly over the past 75 years, as has the breadth and depth of public international law. In parallel, the cases that comprise the Court's docket have evolved.

The number and diversity of States that can look to the Court as a forum for the peaceful settlement of inter-State disputes has greatly increased. When the Court held its opening sitting in April 1946, there were only 51 Members of the United Nations. Almost a third of the world's population lived in non-self-governing territories. If we fast forward 75 years, there are now 193 United Nations Member States, each one entitled to sovereign equality. To date, over 100 States have been parties to contentious cases heard by the Court.

Looking back at the cases that have occupied the Court's attention since I was elected to serve as a judge in September 2010, I am encouraged to see that they have arisen from all geopolitical regions of the world. Some cases involve disagreements between neighbours, such as disputes concerning land and maritime boundaries. In some cases, the general relationship between the parties is strained. In other proceedings, States that are close allies find value in settling their differences before the Court. In this respect, the founders' aspiration to create a real World Court for all nations has been fulfilled.

There is also increased variety in the issues of law and fact presented to the Court, reflecting both developments in international law and the legal questions that are of greatest concern to individual States, and to organs of the United Nations at particular points in time. The Court has proven to be well equipped to address both traditional and newer areas of international law on the basis of its Statute, which has never been amended or revised during the Court's history. Credit is due to the prescience of the Statute's drafters, who struck the right balance between prescribing the infrastructure for the Court's work, while at the same time allowing sufficient flexibility to ensure its continued relevance in decades to come.

The drafters were bold in creating a standing, global forum for the settlement of inter-State disputes on any topic governed by international law. However, they were also circumspect: the Statute does not prescribe the content of international

The Court in session in the Great Hall of Justice.

law to be applied by the Court, but instead leaves it to be developed elsewhere, for example in treaties. This has enabled the Court to settle disputes and render advisory opinions relating to all fields of public international law, including new areas that have emerged and developed since its first sitting. For instance, as environmental risks have become more apparent and their management more complex, the Court has been called upon to deal with a number of disputes involving the environment. In recent years, it has received high marks in particular for the way it has handled the scientific and technical questions that inevitably arise in such cases.

The substance of international law today is not only broader but also deeper than it was when the Court was established. In 1946, public international law consisted primarily of a bundle of "horizontal" obligations owed by States to other States. With the development of international human rights law over the following decades, international law has increasingly governed States' treatment of their own populations. In a number of judgments and advisory opinions, the Court has addressed human rights law and international humanitarian law, which applies in situations of armed conflict. In those proceedings, States and organs of the United Nations may be the participants in the Great Hall of Justice, but the dignity and rights of human beings are at the centre of the Court's inquiry.

A further achievement that should not be overlooked is the Court's development, over the past 75 years, of a significant body of jurisprudence. Judgments of the Court bind only the parties to a particular case. In this respect, the Court differs from the courts of common law countries, which not only settle disputes but also make law that is generally binding. Nonetheless, one of the ideas behind the establishment of a permanent forum for the settlement of inter-State disputes was that "the Court . . . being composed of judges, permanently associated with each other in the same work, . . . retaining their seats from one case to another, can develop a continuous tradition, and assure the harmonious and logical development of International Law" (Final report of the Advisory Committee of Jurists, 24 July 1920). The drafters of the Court's Statute recognized that the Court's pronouncements on the law would provide guidance to all States, as well as to international organizations and scholars. The reach of the Court's jurisprudence is facilitated by the transparent way in which the ICJ operates. Whereas international arbitration traditionally takes place in private, the ICJ's hearings and written proceedings are publicly available, most recently through the Court's website. The Court's decisions are frequently invoked by States in disputes and international negotiations, analysed in depth by commentators, and cited by domestic, regional and international judicial bodies.

With respect to the Court's procedures, the Statute sets out the fundamental principles, ensuring the predictability and fairness of the Court's proceedings, while leaving the detailed rules to be fleshed out — and, when necessary, updated — by the judges. This procedural flexibility has enabled the Court to adapt its methods of work to new and unforeseeable circumstances, most recently the onset of the COVID-19 pandemic. Certainly, the drafters of the ICJ Statute would not have imagined that the Great Hall of Justice, 75 years after the Court's first solemn sitting, would host hybrid hearings in which parties, counsel and judges participate from locations around the world via video link. They would nonetheless have been pleased to know that the Court has met the challenges of the current pandemic and has continued its important work, by taking full advantage of new technologies, while remaining faithful to the imperative of procedural fairness.

The impetus for the establishment of a World Court was the hope that States would settle their disputes before international judges on the basis of law, rather than through force. That was an ambitious goal in 1946, as it remains today. While the creation of the United Nations, including its principal judicial organ, did not put an end to war, in the ensuing 75 years international adjudication has come to occupy an established place in world affairs. Not only has the ICJ been active, but States have also established and reinvigorated a number of other international and regional courts and tribunals, each with a specific mandate to settle certain kinds of disputes peacefully and under international law. These developments give rise to what I regard as a healthy element of competition among dispute settlement bodies. No international court or tribunal can simply rest on its laurels, and the International Court of Justice has no intention of doing so. Instead, on its seventy-fifth anniversary, the Court stands ready to fulfil its mission and thus, as Sir Hersch Lauterpacht put it in 1958, to serve as "one of the instruments for securing peace in so far as this aim can be achieved through law". •

Judge Joan E. Donoghue
President

C. P. J. I.
A/B 56
C. P. J. I.
1923.
Le 17 août.
Dossier E. b. II.
Rôle III. 1.
COUR PERMANENTE DE JUSTICE INTERNATIONALE
ARRÊT N° 1.
AFFAIRE DU VAPEUR «WIMBLEDON».
1923.
August 17th.
File E. b. II.
Docket III. 1.
PERMANENT COURT OF INTERNATIONAL JUSTICE.
JUDGMENT No. 1.
THE S.S. "WIMBLEDON".

THE HISTORY OF THE "WORLD COURT"

The International Court of Justice was born out of decades-long efforts to develop peaceful means to resolve international disputes.

The modern history of international dispute settlement is generally recognized as dating from the Treaty of Amity, Commerce and Navigation, signed between the United States and Great Britain in 1794. This treaty — also known as the Jay Treaty after American negotiator John Jay, Chief Justice of the US Supreme Court — provided for the creation of three mixed commissions composed of equal numbers of American and British nationals, whose task was to settle several outstanding questions arising from the American War of Independence which had proved impossible to resolve through negotiation. The Jay Treaty signalled to the international community that using a peaceful mechanism to resolve an international dispute was a viable alternative to armed conflict.

Another decisive moment in the development of peaceful dispute settlement mechanisms was the 1872 *Alabama Claims* arbitration between Great Britain and the United States. In 1871, the two countries signed the Treaty of Washington, in which they agreed to submit to an arbitration tribunal US claims that Great Britain had violated neutrality during the American Civil War by allowing several warships, including the *Alabama*, to be constructed and sold to Confederate states. The 1871 Treaty provided that the tribunal was to consist of five arbitrators, who would be appointed by the Heads of State of the two parties and by those of three non-party States, namely Brazil, Italy and Switzerland. In its award, the tribunal found that Great Britain had failed to fulfil its duties in respect of the *Alabama* and other ships, and ordered it to pay compensation to the United States. The award was duly implemented and a sum of US$15,500,000 paid in gold by Great Britain to the United States. The proceedings served to demonstrate that arbitration was effective in settling major disputes, and led to a move towards international arbitration at the end of the nineteenth century.

The First Hague Peace Conference and the creation of the Permanent Court of Arbitration

The First Hague Peace Conference of 1899 was convened at the initiative of Russian Tsar Nicholas II and marked the beginning of the next phase in the development of international arbitration. Its main aim was to discuss peace and disarmament. Smaller European States, some Asian States and Mexico were among the participants, which was remarkable for the time.

The Conference lasted for two months and culminated in the adoption of a Final Act containing the following three conventions:

- the Convention for the Pacific Settlement of International Disputes (Convention I);
- the Convention with Respect to the Laws and Customs of War on Land (Convention II); and
- the Convention for the Adaptation to Maritime Warfare of the Principles of the Geneva Convention (Convention III).

First judgment rendered by the PCIJ in the S.S. "Wimbledon" case.

The Convention for the Pacific Settlement of International Disputes was signed by all 26 States represented at the Conference. Its adoption proved to be a significant achievement. Although the participants failed to reach an agreement on the establishment of a true world court with a permanent bench, the Convention did provide for the creation of a lasting mechanism, the Permanent Court of Arbitration (PCA), which would facilitate the establishment and work of arbitral tribunals.

The PCA was established in 1899 and began operating in 1900. It is still active today.

The Second Hague Peace Conference

The Second Hague Peace Conference of 1907 was first proposed by US President Theodore Roosevelt and hosted delegates from 44 States, including from Central and South America. It aimed to deal with issues left unresolved by the First Hague Peace Conference, and was another important milestone for international law and diplomacy.

Several participants believed that the Conference should focus on matters beyond improving the mechanisms established in 1899, and the United States, the United Kingdom and Germany submitted a joint proposal for the creation of a permanent court with full-time judges, devoted to the resolution of international disputes through judicial means. Sadly, the Conference was unable to reach agreement on the proposal, and it became apparent in the course of the discussions that one of the major obstacles to creating a world court was finding an acceptable selection process for its judges.

In the end, the Conference confined itself to recommending that States should adopt a draft convention for the creation of a court of arbitral justice, once an agreement was reached on "the selection of the judges and the constitution of the court". Although this court was never to see the light of day, the draft convention enshrined certain fundamental ideas that some years later would serve as the basis of the Statute of the Permanent Court of International Justice.

The creation of the League of Nations

In January 1919, in the wake of the First World War, the victorious allied forces met at the Paris Peace Conference to negotiate a settlement framework for the defeated powers. American President Woodrow Wilson chaired the committee tasked with drawing up a list of "rules and regulations" for the creation of an international organization whose purpose was to preserve world peace.

The resulting document was the draft of an agreement or covenant between nations whose mission was to maintain world peace. Less than four months later, on 29 April 1919, the final version of the Covenant of the League of Nations was adopted.

The Covenant outlined the basic objectives of the League of Nations, namely to ensure collective security, promote co-operation between States and guarantee the application of peace treaties.

The League of Nations was officially inaugurated on 10 January 1920, and between 1920 and 1939 some 63 countries became members.

The founding of the Permanent Court of International Justice

The Covenant of the League of Nations provided for the establishment of a Permanent Court of International Justice (PCIJ), with jurisdiction to deal with disputes submitted to it by States and to give advisory opinions on questions referred to it by the Council or Assembly of the League of Nations. In 1920, the Council of the League appointed an Advisory Committee of Jurists to prepare a report on the establishment of the PCIJ. The Committee, which met in The Hague, submitted its report in August 1920. On that basis, the Council prepared a draft statute for consideration by the Assembly of the League. In December 1920, the Assembly unanimously adopted the Statute of the PCIJ, the first international judicial tribunal.

As in arbitral proceedings, the jurisdiction of the PCIJ depended on the parties' willingness to refer a dispute to it. However, under

First Hague Peace Conference	Second Hague Peace Conference	Adoption of the Statute of the Permanent Court of International Justice	Inaugural sitting of the Permanent Court of International Justice	Creation of the United Nations and the International Court of Justice	Inaugural sitting of the International Court of Justice
1899	1907	1920	1922	1945	1947

Article 36 of the PCIJ Statute, a State could declare beforehand that it recognized the compulsory jurisdiction of the Court to entertain any future dispute with any other State having made the same declaration.

This new development meant that a State could seise the Court unilaterally, summoning another State to appear before it, without having to reach a prior agreement with that State to submit the dispute in question to the Court. The PCIJ also broke new ground in other respects:

- It was a permanently constituted body, governed by its Statute and Rules of Procedure, established beforehand and binding on parties having recourse to it.
- It had a permanent Registry which, among other things, served as a channel of communication with governments and international bodies.
- It was empowered to give advisory opinions on any dispute or question referred to it by the Council or Assembly of the League of Nations.
- It could develop a constant practice and maintain a certain continuity in its decisions, enabling it to make a greater contribution to the development of international law.
- Its proceedings were largely public.

Although the Court was founded and financed by the League of Nations, it was not a part of the League, and its Statute, contained in a separate protocol, never formed part of the Covenant of the League of Nations. A Member State was therefore not automatically a party to the PCIJ's Statute.

Over time, however, adherence to the Court's compulsory jurisdiction became widespread among States, and several hundred treaties were signed during the 1920s and beyond conferring jurisdiction on the PCIJ in the event of a dispute. The PCIJ proved to be an outstanding success: between 1922 and 1940, it rendered 32 judgments in contentious cases between States and gave 27 advisory opinions. The Court thus made an important, and unprecedented, contribution to the development of international law.

The outbreak of the Second World War in 1939 brought an abrupt end to the PCIJ's activities. After holding its last public sitting on 4 December 1939 and delivering its final order on 26 February 1940, the PCIJ closed its doors as judicial business was largely suspended. A single judge and a skeleton staff of Dutch Registry officials remained in The Hague, while the rest of the Court relocated from its seat at the Peace Palace to Geneva, to wait out the darkest hours of the war.

The establishment of the United Nations and the International Court of Justice

In October 1943, the Ministers for Foreign Affairs of China, the Soviet Union, the United Kingdom and the United States met in Moscow to promote co-operation between their governments and to discuss the measures to be taken to bring an end to the Second World War and ensure a future, lasting peace.

At the conclusion of the Moscow Conference, the participating governments adopted a Joint Four-Nation Declaration called the Moscow Declaration, recognizing the need to establish "at the earliest practicable date a general international organization, based on the principle of the sovereign equality of all peace-loving States, and open to membership by all such States, large and small, for the maintenance of international peace and security".

The Moscow Declaration led to further exchanges between the four powers at Dumbarton Oaks in October 1944, which resulted in the publication of proposals for the establishment of a post-war international organization. These proposals were submitted by the four powers to the governments and peoples of all countries for review. The principal bodies of the proposed international organization included a General Assembly, a Security Council, a Secretariat and an International Court of Justice.

The following year, 850 delegates, advisers and staff from 50 countries, representing some 80 per cent of the world's population, met at the 1945 San Francisco Conference. Based on the Dumbarton Oaks proposals, a final Charter, acceptable to all,

1976	1978	1999	2013	2020	2021
Adoption of the Resolution concerning the Internal Judicial Practice of the Court	Adoption of the new Rules of Court	Launch of the Judicial Fellowship Programme	100th anniversary of the Peace Palace	First hearings by video link	The Court celebrates its 75th anniversary

was finally drafted and signed on 26 June 1945 by representatives from all 50 countries.

On 24 October 1945, once the Charter had been ratified by China, France, the Soviet Union, the United Kingdom and the United States, and by a majority of other signatories, the United Nations officially came into existence.

The 1945 San Francisco Conference also gave birth to the ICJ, which was established under the UN Charter as one of the six main organs and the principal judicial organ of the United Nations. The Statute of the Court is annexed to the Charter, of which it forms an integral part. The Court's integration in the architecture of the United Nations is reflected in its membership and composition, and in its relations with other United Nations organs:

- Under the UN Charter, all Members of the United Nations are *ipso facto* parties to the Court's Statute and agree to comply with the decision of the Court in any case to which they are a party.
- The judges of the Court are elected by United Nations Member States, through the General Assembly and the Security Council.
- The Court's mandate is complementary to the work carried out by the other principal organs of the United Nations.

At its final session in October 1945, the PCIJ decided to transfer all its archives and effects to the ICJ, which was also to have its seat at the Peace Palace in The Hague. On 31 January 1946, the judges of the PCIJ resigned, and on 6 February 1946, the United Nations General Assembly and Security Council elected the first Members of the ICJ.

In April of that year, meeting for the first time, the ICJ elected as its President Judge José Gustavo Guerrero (El Salvador), who had been the last President of the PCIJ. After appointing the members of its Registry (largely from among former officials of the PCIJ), the Court held its inaugural public sitting on 18 April 1946.

Head of the United States delegation addressing delegates at the San Francisco Conference.

The ICJ: 1946 to the present day

Initial interest in referring cases to the Court was slow. Its first case, the *Corfu Channel* case, which concerned State responsibility for damage at sea and was brought by the United Kingdom against Albania, was not submitted until May 1947. That same year the General Assembly adopted a resolution emphasizing the need to make greater use of the ICJ, after which the Court's workload increased to a rate comparable to that of the PCIJ, with an average of two to three new cases per year throughout the 1950s, mostly relating to questions of territorial delimitation and diplomatic protection.

The 1960s saw a dramatic decrease in the number of cases submitted to the ICJ, and between July 1962 and January 1967, and February 1967 and August 1971, no new cases were brought at all.

The situation changed during the late 1970s, as the Court began to consider disputes directly affecting international peace and security, marking a renewed interest in its work. Confidence in the Court increased during the 1980s and 1990s, when it was asked to rule on an ever-growing number of legal questions arising from past or ongoing armed conflicts and large-scale humanitarian crises. Over the last 20 years, the Court's judicial activity has remained at a very high level, and new challenges facing the international community, such as the protection of common resources, have appeared on its docket.

During its 75 years of existence, the Court has had to adapt to major developments in international relations, and an examination of the cases on its docket reveals the growing range of issues on which it has been called to rule. For a long time, the Court dealt primarily with questions of territorial and maritime boundaries; in recent years, however, it has entertained cases concerning the preservation of the marine environment, the protection of international watercourses, the legality of the use of nuclear weapons, the protection of shared or common resources, diplomatic protection and immunities, genocide, State responsibility, reparations and racial discrimination, to name but a few.

The Court, which was originally open to 51 States, now has 193 States parties to its Statute, more than half of which have appeared in contentious proceedings before it. In its first 15 years, the States appearing before the Court were mostly European countries and the United States, but are now from all regions of the world.

Growth in number of cases before the Court (1946-2021)

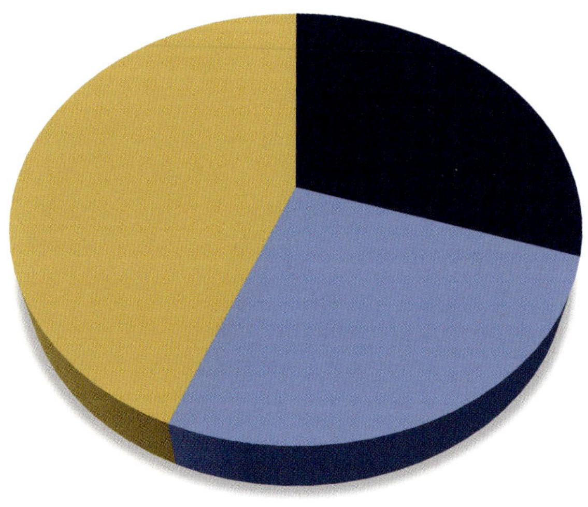

Above, left:
Judge José Gustavo Guerrero, last President of the PCIJ and first President of the ICJ.

Above, right:
Judge Guerrero, presiding in the Panevezys-Saldutiskis Railway case before the PCIJ.

Below, left:
Discussion between the Parties in the Corfu Channel case.

Below, right:
Mine removal in the Corfu Channel, 1946.

PHILIPS

Cape Kephali
GERMAN MINEFIELD
QBY 257
Porto Edda
(Saranda)
NORTH CHANNEL
ROCKY COAST
GERMAN MINEFIELD
QBY 539
Aprau B.
Bolana B.
CORFU
Tetranisi
20°E

THE PEACE PALACE, SEAT OF THE COURT

Built in 1913, the Peace Palace has been the seat of the ICJ since it began its activities in 1946. Located on the outskirts of The Hague's city centre, the Palace sits on five hectares of landscaped grounds which once formed part of the royal estate of Zorgvliet.

In addition to serving as the seat of the ICJ, the Palace is home to the Permanent Court of Arbitration, the Hague Academy of International Law and the Peace Palace Library, one of the world's largest libraries specializing in public international law. The Palace building itself is owned and managed by the Carnegie Foundation.

A "temple of peace"

Following the establishment of the PCA in 1899, the idea of finding it a permanent home began to gain momentum. Andrew Dickson White, American diplomat and delegate at the First Hague Peace Conference, and Friedrich Fromhold Martens, Russian diplomat and jurist, who represented Russia at both Hague Peace Conferences, were among those who were instrumental in persuading the Scottish-American steel magnate and philanthropist Andrew Carnegie to fund the construction of a "temple of peace" fit to house the PCA.

On 15 August 1905, a major international competition was launched to find a suitable design for the "Peace Palace". By the time the competition closed almost one year later, 216 entries comprising over 3,000 drawings had been received, including one from the renowned Dutch architect Hendrik Petrus Berlage, whose later works included The Hague's Kunstmuseum (formerly known as the Gemeentemuseum).

Six prize winners were identified by the jury, with first prize going, somewhat controversially, to the French architect Louis Cordonnier of Lille. His design sparked fierce debate among the jury members and the general public, many of whom had hoped for a more contemporary building than the neo-renaissance-inspired palace envisioned by the Frenchman.

A few compromises were necessary, however, to bring Cordonnier's original design within the US$1.5-million budget donated by Carnegie (US$46 million in today's money). Cordonnier was obliged to modify his plans, reducing the number of towers from four to two and removing other expensive features such as a separate library, which was eventually incorporated into the main building itself. The design of the Palace was finalized in collaboration with the Dutch architect Johan van der Steur, who was later appointed executive architect for the construction phase.

Midway through the Second Hague Peace Conference of 1907, the first stone of the Peace Palace was laid. Remarkably, construction took only six years to complete. A ceremony to inaugurate the Peace Palace was held on 28 August 1913, in the presence of the Dutch royal family, Andrew Carnegie and international jurists, politicians and pacifist groups.

Detail from the stained-glass windows in the Great Hall of Justice, "Evolution of the Peace Ideal", by Scottish artist Douglas Strachan.

French architect Louis Cordonnier's original design for the Peace Palace.

The Peace Palace under construction.

The building's first occupant, the PCA, was soon joined by the Permanent Court of International Justice, the ICJ's predecessor, which shared the Peace Palace with the PCA from 1922 until 1946, when the PCIJ was dissolved. The ICJ began its work that same year and has occupied the former PCIJ premises in the Peace Palace ever since.

A tour of the Palace

As a sign of their support for the ideals of peace embodied by the Peace Palace, many of the nations that had attended the Second Hague Peace Conference donated items to be used in the construction and decoration of this iconic building. The iron gates at the entrance to the grounds, with their bronze medallions depicting the goddesses Amicitia, Concordia, Pax and Justitia, were designed by the German architect Bruno Möhring and donated by Germany in 1912. They are supported by sandstone pillars decorated with angels, cherubs and vines. Granite donated by Norway was used for driveways and for the stairs leading to the entrance of the Palace.

The Palace itself sits on a base of granite donated by Sweden and its façades feature Dutch red brick and decorative elements made of natural stone, including sandstone. The building's two towers mark the locations of its courtrooms: the larger tower stands above the Small Hall of Justice, currently used by the PCA, and the smaller tower crowns the Great Hall of Justice, the courtroom of the ICJ.

The clock on the large tower, donated by Switzerland in 1912, is engraved with the fitting message "Möchte ich mit meinem Geläute den aufrichtigen Frieden verkünden", which can be roughly translated as "May my chime be the announcement of a lasting peace". The tower also houses a 48-bell carillon that can often be heard throughout the surrounding neighbourhood.

On entering the Palace through its massive iron doors — a gift from Belgium — visitors are immediately struck by the building's eclectic mix of decorative styles.

View of the Peace Palace bell tower and inner courtyard.

Much of the Palace's interior was designed by the 24-year-old Dutch architect and designer Herman Rosse, who was heavily influenced by the Arts and Crafts movement. Rosse employed a team of artisans to decorate large expanses of the Palace's interior walls with hand-crafted images of flora and fauna carefully interwoven with symbols of peace and justice, while the Dutch pottery firms Rozenburg and Porceleyne Fles were commissioned to produce the countless wall tiles that feature throughout the building. Rosse's most remarkable work, however, can be found just above the grand staircase: a breath-taking gilt ceiling depicting the goddesses of peace, law, order and justice.

Marble statue "Peace through Justice" by American sculptor Andrew O'Connor.

The entrance hall features a series of imposing columns and pillars, which, along with the floors, are predominantly made from marble donated by Italy (including Arabescato and Yellow Sienna marble). The floors are also interlaid with small amounts of Belgian blue stone set in geometric patterns. The large majolica vases on either side of the entrance hall, donated by Hungary, bear images of lions and owls, symbols of strength and wisdom.

At the centre of the entrance hall is the grand staircase, a replica of the stairs at the Opera Garnier in Paris, donated by the municipality of The Hague. On either side of the stairs, wood-panelled doors lead to two identical meeting rooms used by parties when they come to the Court for hearings.

A marble statue entitled "Peace through Justice", created by the American sculptor Andrew O'Connor and donated by the United States, sits in the alcove halfway up the stairs. The statue depicts a modern Lady Justice who has cast off her blindfold, scales and sword. Five porcelain vases donated by the municipality of Amsterdam surround the statue, representing, from left to right, the Huis ten Bosch (the site of the First Hague Peace Conference), the initials of Tsar Nicholas II (the initiator of the First Hague Peace Conference), Groenburgwal (a canal in Amsterdam), the initials of Queen Wilhelmina (who hosted the First Hague Peace Conference) and the Vijverberg (the seat of the Dutch Government).

Seven large stained-glass windows, designed by Adolf Le Comte and produced by the Schouten Studio of Delft, light up the alcove. The two outermost windows depict war and the scourges of humanity, while the five central windows portray the virtues of peace, with the sun goddess in the centre, casting peaceful rays of light over Earth.

Donated by Austria, six large gilded-bronze chandeliers trimmed with semi-precious stones and Bohemian crystal bedeck the staircase.

Overlooking the alcove is a statue donated by Argentina entitled "Christ of the Andes". It is a replica of the statue which stands on the border between Chile and Argentina as a symbol of peace

A majolica vase in the entrance hall.

The Great Hall of Justice.

between the two countries, which were on the brink of war at the beginning of the twentieth century. Their dispute was ultimately resolved peacefully with the help of Edward VII.

The Great Hall of Justice, which in the past was used by the PCIJ and the PCA, now serves as the courtroom of the ICJ. This grand room features four large stained-glass windows created by the Scottish artist Douglas Strachan and donated by the United Kingdom. They depict the "Evolution of the Peace Ideal" in four stages, from the primitive age to the age of conquest, the present age and, finally, peace achieved, in which humanity lives harmoniously together.

A large painting entitled "Paix par la Justice" ("Peace through Justice"), by the French artist Albert Besnard, sits above the doorway through which the judges enter the Great Hall at the start of public sittings.

At the centre of the painting is Irene, goddess of peace, holding in her arms a child, the god Pluto. She stands between two warring parties, and on the rocks above her are two arbiters on either side of an umpire.

Adjacent to the Great Hall are the Red and Green Rooms. Before public sittings of the Court, Members first enter the Green Room, or "robing room", where they dress in plain black robes with white jabots made of Belgian lace. The room is lined with portraits of former Members of the PCIJ. The first portrait on the left on entering the Red Room — where the judges meet during Court sittings — is that of President José Gustavo Guerrero, the last President of the PCIJ and the first President of the ICJ.

Surprisingly to many, ICJ judges do not have their offices in the Peace Palace itself. Instead, it is the staff members of the Court's Registry who enjoy these beautiful surroundings. The offices of the judges and their teams are tucked away from view in the Judges' Wing, which is nestled in the trees behind the Peace Palace. This "New Wing" is also the site of the ICJ's deliberation room.

The Judges' Wing was designed by Jaap Schrieke of the architecture firm Deurvorst & Schrieke. Construction began in 1975, and in 1978 the wing was inaugurated by Queen Juliana, in the presence of the then United Nations Secretary-General, Kurt Waldheim. Work on an extension to the New Wing began in early 1992, on account of the ICJ's growing workload, and was completed in 1997. The building is a veritable treasure trove of gifts donated by visiting Heads of State and other high-ranking officials over the Court's 75 years of existence.

The Peace Palace gardens

In 1908, a competition was launched to design the Peace Palace gardens. Three garden designers were invited to submit proposals; the top prize was awarded to the Englishman Thomas Mawson, who was known for designs in which "garden and building form a unity". The final design, which had to be simplified for financial reasons, included a rosarium and a large pond created from a diverted natural water course located in the nearby dunes. It also featured spacious terraces built from the same materials as the Palace, creating a subtle connection between the two.

Mawson carefully selected plants that represent peace, and tried to avoid those with sharp thorns, with the exception of roses, which symbolize love. Only trees and shrubs with small leaves were used in order to allow as much light as possible into the garden. Shielded from the bustle of the city by tall, old trees which previously formed part of the Zorgvliet estate, the Palace gardens remain an oasis of peace and tranquillity. •

Side view of the Peace Palace, Judges' Wing, gardens and pond.

COUR INTERNATIONALE DE JUSTICE
INTERNATIONAL COURT OF JUSTICE

THE COMPOSITION OF THE COURT

The ICJ is composed of 15 independent judges, also referred to by the Court's Statute as "Members of the Court", elected for a term of office of nine years. To ensure continuity within the Court, one third of its membership (five judges) is elected every three years. Elections are held during the annual session of the United Nations General Assembly, which takes place in New York each autumn. Members may be re-elected on the expiry of their terms and, unlike in some national legal systems, they are not subject to an age limit or compulsory retirement age. To safeguard their independence, Members of the Court cannot be dismissed unless the other judges unanimously agree that they no longer fulfil the required conditions.

Nomination of candidates and elections

The means by which candidates become Members of the Court is different from the process followed in many domestic legal systems, where judges may, for instance, be appointed by the executive or legislative branch of the State or, in some countries, by the judiciary itself.

Candidates for election to the Court are not proposed directly by United Nations Member States, nor are they nominated by the Court. They are elected by the General Assembly and the Security Council from a list of persons nominated by the "national groups" in the Permanent Court of Arbitration; these groups are composed of individuals designated as potential arbitrators by each Contracting Party of the PCA. The ICJ's Statute sets out a similar nomination process for United Nations Member States not represented in the PCA.

At least three months before the elections, the United Nations Secretary-General asks the national groups to nominate candidates for election to the ICJ. Each group may nominate up to four persons, no more than two of whom may be of the group's nationality. Before putting forward candidates, national groups are advised to consult their highest courts of justice, legal faculties and schools of law, and members of law academies. A list of nominees is then prepared by the Secretary-General for submission to the General Assembly and the Security Council.

Each of these organs proceeds to elect Members of the Court simultaneously but independently. In the General Assembly, all United Nations Member States and States parties to the Court's Statute are entitled to cast votes. Voting in the Security Council takes place without distinction between permanent and non-permanent members. This means that no permanent member of the Security Council can "veto" the outcome of the vote in the Council. To be elected, a candidate must obtain an absolute majority of votes in both the General Assembly and the Security Council, which may require successive rounds of voting over the course of several meetings. If one or more seats remain unfilled after three meetings held for the purpose of the elections, a joint conference consisting of six members — three appointed by the General Assembly and three by the Security Council — may be formed to propose one name for each vacant seat, which is then submitted for approval by both organs. To date, however, this mechanism has never been used.

The full Court.

Members of the Court, composition as at 6 February 2021

President
Joan E. Donoghue

(United States of America)

Vice-President
Kirill Gevorgian

(Russian Federation)

Judge
Peter Tomka

(Slovakia)

Judge
Ronny Abraham

(France)

Judge
Mohamed Bennouna

(Morocco)

Judge
Antônio Augusto
Cançado Trindade
(Brazil)

Judge
Abdulqawi Ahmed Yusuf

(Somalia)

Judge
Xue Hanqin

(China)

Judge
Julia Sebutinde

(Uganda)

Judge
Dalveer Bhandari

(India)

Judge
Patrick Lipton Robinson

(Jamaica)

Judge
James Richard Crawford

(Australia)

Judge
Nawaf Salam

(Lebanon)

Judge
Iwasawa Yuji

(Japan)

Judge
Georg Nolte

(Germany)

Registrar
Philippe Gautier

(Belgium)

Diversity and geographical representation

In electing Members of the Court, voting States are required by the Statute to bear in mind not only that the selected judges should possess the necessary qualifications, but also that the composition of the Court as a whole should represent the world's main forms of civilization and principal legal systems. In accordance with the Statute, judges should be elected from among persons of high moral character who have the qualifications required in their respective countries for appointment to the highest judicial offices, or who are of recognized competence in the field of international law.

To reflect the diversity of United Nations membership, the election of judges also takes into account the need for equitable geographical distribution. The Statute of the Court stipulates that no two Members should be nationals of the same State. Since 1946, the Court's composition has generally had the following regional distribution:

- three judges from the Group of African States;
- three judges from the Group of Asia-Pacific States;
- two judges from the Group of Eastern European States;
- two judges from the Group of Latin American and Caribbean States; and
- five judges from the Western European and Other States Group.

It may be noted, however, that as of February 2018, the Court includes four judges from the Western European and Other States Group and four from the Group of Asia-Pacific States.

Throughout its history, the Court has had on its Bench nationals of the five permanent members of the Security Council — China, France, Russia, the United Kingdom and the United States — with two exceptions: from 1967 to 1984, there was no judge of Chinese nationality, and since 2018, there has been no judge from the United Kingdom.

Election of Members of the Court by the UN General Assembly and Security Council.

Role and functions of Members of the Court

The judges elected at the triennial elections held during the General Assembly's autumn session begin their term of office on 6 February of the following year. At the first meeting of the Court in its new composition, the Members elect a President and a Vice-President for a term of three years. The President's role is to preside over all hearings and meetings of the Court, to direct its work and to supervise its administration, with the assistance of committees composed of Members of the Court. During judicial deliberations, the President has a casting vote in the event of votes being tied. The Vice-President stands in for the President in his or her absence, in the event of a vacancy in the presidency or when the President is unable to exercise his or her functions.

> *I solemnly declare that I will perform my duties and exercise my powers as judge honourably, faithfully, impartially and conscientiously.*

Judge Iwasawa Yuji making his solemn declaration at a public sitting of the Court.

Sitting judges are independent and do not represent or act on behalf of their respective countries or any other State. Before taking up their duties, Members make a solemn declaration in open court (usually at the first public sitting in which they take part) to exercise their powers impartially and conscientiously.

During their term of office, Members may not exercise any political or administrative functions or engage in any other professional occupation. Furthermore, they may not act as agent, counsel or advocate of a party to a case pending before the Court, nor may they participate in the decision of any case in which they have previously taken part, in any capacity. In recent years, the Court has adopted guidelines on the external activities of its Members, including the conditions under which a judge may act as an arbitrator in inter-State arbitration proceedings, engage in teaching activities and academic discussions, publish writings or hold positions in external entities such as learned societies. As a fundamental principle, judicial activities must always take priority over external ones.

Dame Rosalyn Higgins, first female judge and President of the Court.

Various profiles and backgrounds

The judges elected to the Court since 1946 have had varied professional backgrounds and experience and have generally been in the later stages of their careers. Prior to election, some Members have held judicial office or occupied senior positions in the civil service of their respective countries, while others have worked in private practice or academia, sat on the benches of other international courts or tribunals, served as members of bodies of experts on international law, such as the International Law Commission, or undertaken a combination of these professional activities over the course of their careers. In addition, some judges have previously been involved in cases before the ICJ, either as agent or counsel for their governments, or as a judge *ad hoc*. The diverse backgrounds of the Court's Members is one of its strengths and contributes to the confidence and trust that countries around the globe place in the Court as an impartial and independent forum for the settlement of their disputes. Since the Court was established, the majority of its Members have been male. In 1985, Suzanne Bastid of France became the first woman to sit at the Court, as judge *ad hoc* in the case of the *Application for Revision and Interpretation of the Judgment of 24 February 1982 in the Case concerning the* Continental Shelf (Tunisia/Libyan Arab Jamahiriya) *(Tunisia* v. *Libyan Arab Jamahiriya)*. Over the years, four other female judges *ad hoc* have been chosen in cases before the Court: Judge *ad hoc* Christine van den Wyngaert (Belgium), Judge *ad hoc* Hilary Charlesworth (Australia), Judge *ad hoc* Louise Arbour (Canada) and Judge *ad hoc* Navanethem Pillay (South Africa).

The first woman to be elected as a Member of the Court, Judge Rosalyn Higgins, in 1995, was also the first woman to be elected President of the ICJ (2006-2009). On 8 February 2021, Judge Joan E. Donoghue became the second woman in the Court's history to hold this post. Since 2012, female judges have represented one fifth of the Court's Bench (three of 15 judges: Judge Julia Sebutinde of Uganda, Judge Joan E. Donoghue of the United States and Judge Xue Hanqin of China). While the number of female judges on the Bench remains low, it has tripled since 2006.

In order to ensure their independence and impartiality, Members of the Court enjoy diplomatic privileges and immunities while engaged in the business of the Court. They receive an annual salary and other entitlements, the amounts and conditions of which are fixed by the General Assembly.

Judges *ad hoc*

Members of the Court who are a national of a State party to a case before the Court are not disqualified from sitting in the case. However, in order to ensure equality between the parties to the case, if a State party has no judge of its nationality on the Bench, it may choose a person to sit as judge *ad hoc*. For example, in the *Jadhav* case between India and Pakistan, where the Bench included a national of India but not one of Pakistan, the latter was entitled to choose a judge *ad hoc*. In the *Arrest Warrant of 11 April 2000* case between the Democratic Republic of the Congo and Belgium, neither State had a judge of its nationality on the Bench, so both parties could choose judges *ad hoc* in the case.

A State party may choose as judge *ad hoc* one of its nationals or a person who has the nationality of another State, even if it is shared by another Member of the Court. For instance, in the case concerning the *Application of the International Convention on the Elimination of All Forms of Racial Discrimination (Qatar* v. *United Arab Emirates)*, each State party chose a French national as judge *ad hoc*. As a result, three French judges sat in the case, since the Court already included a Member of French nationality.

Once appointed, judges *ad hoc* participate in decision-making in the case on equal terms with the other judges. The role of a judge *ad hoc* is not to argue the case for the choosing State, but to ensure that that State's position and arguments are duly taken into consideration in the decision-making process. A judge *ad hoc* is an independent judge who may vote against the choosing State in the decision of the Court — a situation which has happened on several occasions in the Court's history.

The composition of the Court may thus vary from one case to another, and the number of judges sitting in a given case will not necessarily be 15. There may be as many as 16 or 17 judges in cases where judges *ad hoc* have been appointed, or fewer than 15 where one or more elected judges do not sit in the case. A minimum of nine judges is necessary to constitute the Court.

Chambers

The Court can also sit in smaller numbers if a State party to a case requests that it be heard before a chamber. There are three types of chambers at the Court. The Chamber of Summary Procedure, composed of five judges, is constituted annually by the Court with a view to the speedy dispatch of business. A Special Chamber, composed of at least three elected judges, can be constituted to deal with particular categories of disputes, such as those relating to labour, communications or the environment. The third type of chamber, composed of at least three elected judges, may be formed on an *ad hoc* basis to deal with a particular case. The composition of *ad hoc* chambers is decided by the Court after consultation with the States parties to the case.

Although no case has ever been dealt with by the first two types of chambers, *ad hoc* chambers have been constituted in six cases, the majority of which concerned land and maritime boundary disputes. A judgment given by any of the three chambers is considered to be rendered by the full Court. While proceedings before a chamber may offer certain advantages, such as the swift disposal of the case and the possibility of adopting simplified procedures, the use of chambers has remained rather exceptional in the practice of the Court. •

Ms Suzanne Bastid, first female judge ad hoc *to serve at the Court.*

Judge ad hoc Raúl Vinuesa, chosen by Argentina in the Pulp Mills case.

THE REGISTRY OF THE COURT

The Registry is the name given to the Court's secretariat, a permanent administrative office that provides a range of support to the judges in the fulfilment of their duties. It assists the Court in both judicial and diplomatic matters, and performs the linguistic, administrative and financial tasks essential to its functioning. It is headed by a Registrar, who is assisted by a Deputy-Registrar. Both are elected by the Court for a term of seven years. The current Registrar is Mr. Philippe Gautier, of Belgian nationality, and the current Deputy-Registrar is Mr. Jean-Pelé Fomété, of Cameroonian nationality. Before taking up their posts at the helm of the Registry, Mr. Gautier was Registrar of the International Tribunal for the Law of the Sea, while Mr. Fomété served as Programme Director in the Registry of the International Criminal Tribunal for Rwanda.

Organization of the Registry

When the Registry was first formed in 1946, it consisted of a small group of officials who were expected to be "generalists", capable of undertaking legal research, preparing translations and carrying out diplomatic tasks on a day-to-day basis. As the Registry has grown, however, its officials have become more specialized. This is reflected in its current structure — in place since the 1990s — comprising three departments (the Department of Legal Matters, the Department of Linguistic Matters and the Information Department) and eight technical divisions (the Archives, Indexing and Distribution Division, the Finance Division, the Publications Division, the Security and General Assistance Division, the Documents Division/Library of the Court, the Text Processing and Reproduction Division, the Information and Communications Technology Division and the Administrative and Personnel Division). The size of the staff nonetheless remains modest; the Registry currently comprises 117 posts. Registry staff are hired through competitive recruitment procedures, with most required to have a thorough grasp of both English and French, the two official languages of the Court. Careful consideration is given to geographical distribution and gender balance in the recruitment process.

The tasks undertaken by Registry officials are broadly set out in the Instructions for the Registry, as drawn up and approved by the Court on 20 March 2012. Registry officials are also subject to regularly amended Staff Regulations, which are modelled on the Staff Regulations and Staff Rules of the United Nations.

Why are the Court and its Registry unique?

The Court is the only principal organ of the United Nations to be located outside New York and the only principal organ with a separate registry that does not form part of the Secretariat. This separation is necessary: as the principal judicial organ of the United Nations, it is essential that the Court is able to preserve its judicial and administrative independence. The Court has its seat at the Peace Palace in The Hague, which has been dubbed the "International City of Peace and Justice" on account of the

Official photograph of the ICJ Registry, September 2019.

Organizational chart of the Registry

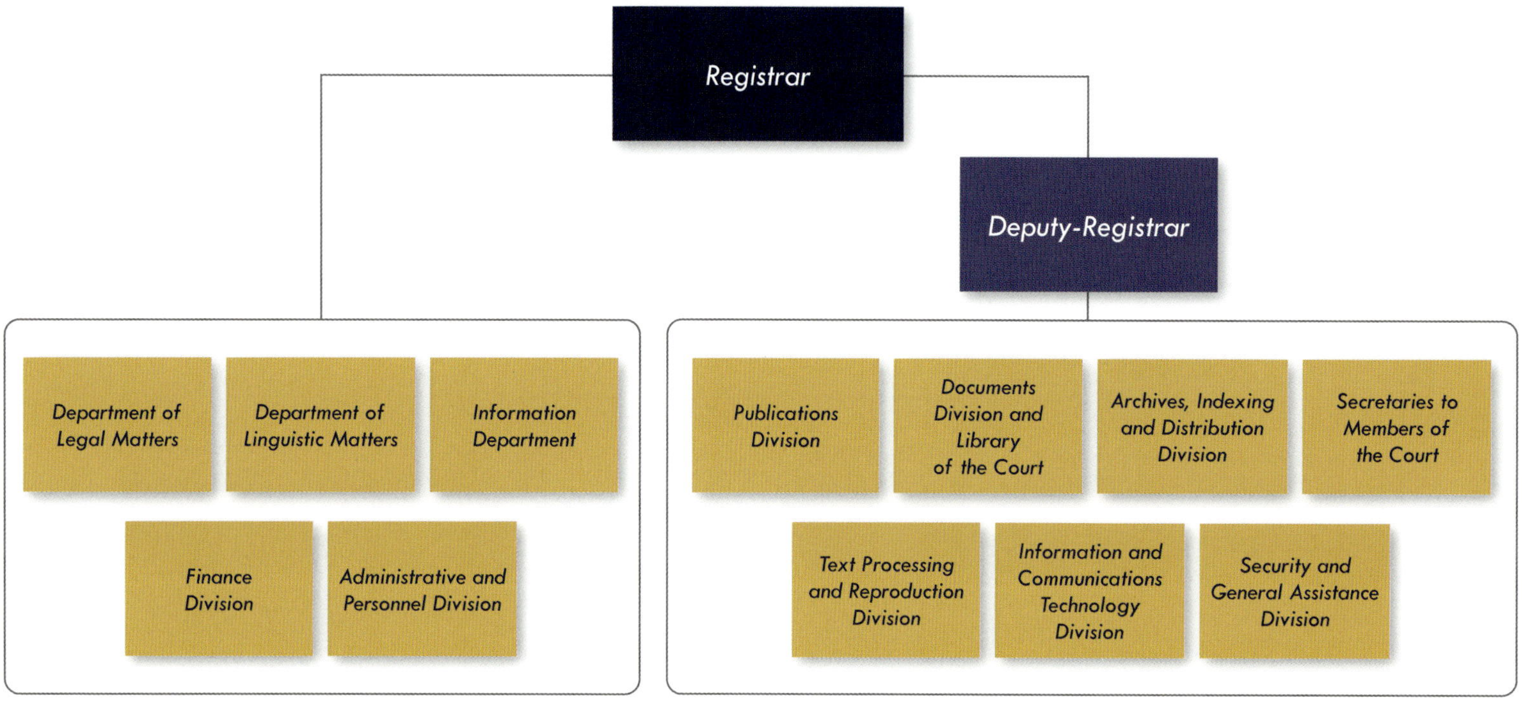

many international law tribunals and international organizations based there. The Hague is thus the duty station of all Registry officials, and the iconic Peace Palace, a symbol of peace and justice, is their place of work.

The role of the different departments and divisions of the Registry

In fulfilling his multiple functions, the Registrar relies on the experience, skill and expertise of the Registry staff.

The Department of Legal Matters

The Department of Legal Matters consists of a core group of eight legal officers, providing legal assistance to both the Court and the Registrar; 15 law clerks, who are assigned to individual judges; and an administrative assistant. The legal officers and law clerks are of an array of nationalities. Their backgrounds are varied: some have prior experience of working in international tribunals, some have experience in private practice in public international law, and others have a background in academia. Many will hold PhDs in international law.

The principal role of the Department of Legal Matters is to provide legal research, drafting and general judicial support to the Court. Legal officers prepare case-related documents to assist the Court in its work, including the procedural history of a case (known as the *"qualités"*), a summary of the arguments put forward by the parties and a list of the legal issues raised. They also draft procedural orders and assist the Court's drafting committees, tasked with preparing draft decisions for consideration and discussion by the full Court. The Department of Legal Matters is responsible for preparing all case-related correspondence. This includes letters to the agents of parties to contentious cases, correspondence with representatives of States participating in advisory proceedings, and any notifications and transmissions provided for in the Statute of the Court. Finally, legal officers attend meetings held by the President and the Registrar with representatives of the parties, and prepare the minutes of the Court's judicial and administrative meetings.

The legal issues raised by the cases before the Court are extremely wide-ranging. Staff members of the Department of Legal Matters must therefore be capable of providing legal support in a variety of areas. Recent cases, for example,

Mr. Philippe Gautier, Registrar, meeting with staff members of the Registry.

A judgment of the Court, signed by the President and the Registrar.

have involved questions of territorial sovereignty, land and maritime boundaries, rights to natural resources, reparations for violations of the principle of non-use of force in international relations, environmental law and international human rights, including the right to consular assistance for detained foreign nationals, and the right to judicial redress for acts of genocide and acts of racial discrimination.

The Department of Linguistic Matters

The Department of Linguistic Matters ensures that all the work of the Court is properly rendered in its two official languages, English and French. It furnishes translations of all official Court documents and many internal documents, provides simultaneous interpretation for public sittings and private meetings of the Court, and offers linguistic advice to the Court and Registry alike.

Unlike other international secretariats where English has become the predominant language, the ICJ has maintained a balance between its two official languages, as required by its Statute. All judgments, advisory opinions and orders are prepared in both languages, from the outset of the drafting process. Deliberations and readings of a draft text are also conducted in both English and French. This bilingualism improves the quality of the legal drafting, since the meaning and structure of a text must pass muster in both languages throughout the drafting process.

Above, left:
UN Secretary-General H.E. Mr. Boutros Boutros-Ghali is welcomed by the President of the Court, Sir Robert Jennings, 20 January 1994.

Above, right:
His Holiness Pope John Paul II addressing the Court, 13 May 1985.

Below, left:
Solemn sitting, 12 April 2006 (left to right: President of the UN General Assembly H.E. Mr. Jan Eliasson, H.M. Queen Beatrix of the Netherlands, Minister for Foreign Affairs of the Netherlands H.E. Mr. Ben Bot, President Rosalyn Higgins and UN Secretary-General H.E. Mr. Kofi Annan).

Below, right:
Visit of the UN Secretary-General, H.E. Mr. António Guterres, to the ICJ, 22 December 2017.

The Information Department

The Information Department is responsible for ensuring that the work of the Court is properly publicized. It is in constant contact with the media and the public, providing information (e.g. through press releases, the website of the Court or social media) on the progress of pending cases. It responds to information requests from diplomatic, legal and academic sources, as well as from the general public. It assists in maintaining relations between the Court and other organs and specialized agencies of the United Nations, as well as international bodies specializing in international law. The Information Department also oversees all protocol matters and is responsible for organizing public hearings and official visits by high-ranking dignitaries.

The Information and Communications Technology Division

The Information and Communications Technology (ICT) Division is responsible for the smooth functioning of the Court's computer systems and electronic resources. It also helps to maintain the Court's website, making sure that the site functions correctly and is easy to access and navigate. More recently, the ICT Division has been instrumental in ensuring that the Court is able to continue to function correctly, through remote meetings and virtual public hearings, when prevented from gathering in person.

The Finance Division

The Finance Division is responsible for the preparation of the Court's draft budget proposals, which are then presented by the Registrar to the budgetary committees in New York, before being examined by the General Assembly. The Finance Division not only prepares the Court's budget estimates, but also ensures that the budget, once approved, is properly implemented, in accordance with the applicable financial regulations and rules.

The Publications Division

The Publications Division is responsible for the publication of various series, in both official languages of the Court, including *Judgments, Advisory Opinions and Orders* and *Pleadings, Oral Arguments, Documents*. Other series include *Acts and Documents*, the *Annuaire-Yearbook* and the *Bibliography of the International Court of Justice* and the Court's *Handbook*, many of which are now available electronically on the Court's website. The Division also produces one-off publications, such as illustrated coffee table books, explaining the Court's role and function to the general public. These books are usually released to coincide with an anniversary or other commemorative event.

The Archives, Indexing and Distribution Division

The Archives, Indexing and Distribution Division is responsible for the storage and digitalization of the Court's documents, including case files and correspondence. This Division plays a key role in document retrieval and storage, and is constantly seeking to apply new technologies to complement its paper records.

The Security and General Assistance Division

The Security and General Assistance Division has responsibility for all security-related matters. It also provides general assistance to Members of the Court and Registry staff in the form of messenger, transport and reception services. It liaises closely with the Carnegie Foundation, which owns the Peace Palace building.

The Documents Division and Library of the Court

The Library dates back to the time of the Permanent Court of International Justice, the ICJ's predecessor. Its collection has grown considerably over the years and now consists of around 60,000 volumes. The Library's main role is to assist Members of the Court and Registry staff with research.

The Text Processing and Reproduction Division

The Text Processing and Reproduction Division provides invaluable support to all departments and divisions of the Registry. It is responsible for ensuring that all Court documents, in both official languages, are produced on time and in accordance with the relevant quality standards.

The Administrative and Personnel Division

The Administrative and Personnel Division has a wide range of duties, including planning and organizing recruitment procedures, the appointment and promotion of staff, and various training opportunities; assisting staff who are separating from service; and managing and overseeing procurement processes.

Other staff members

The Registry also counts among its staff secretaries to judges, the special assistants of the President and the Registrar, various administrative staff serving in the offices of the President, the Registrar and the Deputy-Registrar, a senior medical officer and a staff welfare officer. Every staff member has an important role to play.

The Registry of the Court is made up of a small but dynamic group of dedicated United Nations officials, who work closely together and endeavour to assist the Court as best they can in the fulfilment of its mandate.

Registry staff members.

THE COURT'S JURISDICTION AND THE PRINCIPLE OF CONSENT

The function of the ICJ in contentious cases is to decide in accordance with international law the disputes submitted to it by States. Therefore, it can only deal with a dispute if it is asked to do so by one or more States, and thus it does not decide how many cases are brought before it, what subject-matter they cover or when they are submitted. The Court cannot conduct its own investigations or rule on the actions of States on its own initiative; nor can it resolve all international conflicts, however grave or concerning they may be, since it cannot seise itself of a dispute.

Unlike in the case of other international judicial institutions, acceptance of the Court's jurisdiction is neither automatic nor mandatory for States parties to its Statute. Even as parties to its Statute — through membership of the United Nations or by some other means for which express provision is made — States must consent to the ICJ's jurisdiction over a dispute for the Court to be able to entertain it.

The principle of consent

The ICJ cannot entertain a dispute simply because it has been referred to it by a State: the States parties to the dispute must also have consented to the Court's jurisdiction, i.e. they must agree that the Court can consider the matter at issue. In other words, the States parties to a case must have accepted that the dispute or class of disputes in question may come before the Court. It is this acceptance that determines whether, and to what extent, the Court has jurisdiction to entertain a case submitted to it.

Consent is a fundamental principle of international dispute settlement, according to which no State may be party to a case before the Court unless it has given its agreement. Equal and sovereign, States cannot be brought before an international court or tribunal against their will; they are free to decide whether to settle a dispute and to choose a peaceful means of resolution, be it judicial settlement, negotiation, mediation, conciliation, arbitration or any other means they consider appropriate.

How can consent be expressed?

States can express their consent to the jurisdiction of the Court in several ways and at various times.

They can agree in advance, i.e. before proceedings are instituted before the Court, to accept its jurisdiction in respect of disputes or certain classes of disputes that may arise in the future. This can be done in two ways.

First, States can become parties to a treaty or international agreement concluded by two or more States which contains a clause conferring jurisdiction on the Court in the event of a dispute with another State bound by the same treaty. Such "compromissory clauses" or "jurisdictional clauses" are currently included in more than 300 bilateral and multilateral treaties.

United Nations Secretary-General U Thant receiving the declaration recognizing the compulsory jurisdiction of the Court from Ambassador Simeon Olaosebikan Adebo, Permanent Representative of Nigeria, New York, 3 September 1965.

How can consent to the Court's jurisdiction be expressed?

- Compromissory clause contained in a treaty
- Declaration recognizing the Court's compulsory jurisdiction
- Special agreement
- *Forum prorogatum*

Thus, there are treaties that specifically concern dispute settlement, under whose terms signatory States agree to settle any disputes between them peacefully and which provide for various means of doing so, including through judicial settlement before the Court. Treaties of this type have been concluded at the regional level, for example in the Americas (the 1948 American Treaty on Pacific Settlement, or Pact of Bogotá) and in Europe (the 1957 European Convention for the Peaceful Settlement of Disputes).

Clauses conferring jurisdiction on the Court also appear in treaties whose main object is not dispute settlement, but which concern a range of matters, including environmental law, the protection of human rights, the prevention and punishment of genocide, the prohibition of torture and racial discrimination, economic co-operation and consular relations between States. Such clauses, which can be found in the text of the treaty or in a protocol annexed to it, give States parties to the treaty the possibility of recourse to the Court should they disagree as to how the treaty should be interpreted, for example, or whether a State has complied with its obligations under it. Although their formulation may vary, such clauses usually stipulate that disputes relating to the application or interpretation of the treaty in question may be submitted to the Court for decision.

Some clauses allow States to address the ICJ directly in the event of a dispute; others establish preconditions for its seisin, in particular the obligation for States involved in a dispute to attempt to settle it by other means, such as negotiation, before seising the Court. Compromissory clauses in bilateral or multilateral treaties are currently one of the principal bases of jurisdiction on which disputes are brought before the ICJ.

Second, States can give their consent by making a declaration recognizing the Court's compulsory jurisdiction in respect of any other State having made a similar declaration. As of 1 January 2021, 74 States have made such declarations, which are set out in writing and deposited with the United Nations Secretary-General in New York.

This system of declarations effectively creates a group of States that have mutually given the ICJ jurisdiction to settle any dispute arising between them. In principle, each State in the group is entitled to bring one or more other States in the group before the Court. Conversely, every State that has accepted the Court's compulsory jurisdiction agrees to respect that jurisdiction should proceedings be brought against it by one or more other States having accepted the same obligation.

Declarations accepting the ICJ's jurisdiction are not all worded in the same way, as States are at liberty to determine their content. Some declarations confer very broad jurisdiction on the Court, allowing it to entertain any dispute, without restriction, whereas others narrowly limit the scope of the consent given, making it subject to a series of conditions, also known as "reservations". Declarations may therefore contain reservations intended to limit their application in time (for example by providing that the ICJ has jurisdiction only over disputes arising before or after a certain date) or in space (by excluding disputes involving certain States or territories), or to exclude certain classes of disputes (in particular those which the parties have agreed to resolve by means other

Division of cases based on different bases of jurisdiction

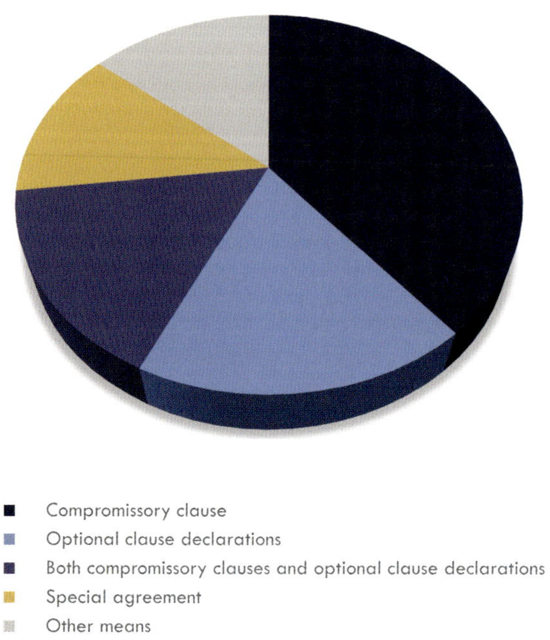

Example text of a declaration recognizing as compulsory the jurisdiction of the International Court of Justice

The Government of STATE recognizes as compulsory ipso facto *and without special agreement, in relation to any other State accepting the same obligation, and on condition of reciprocity, the jurisdiction of the International Court of Justice, in conformity with Article 36, paragraph 2, of the Statute of that Court.*

than the Court, or which relate to particular subjects that, for one reason or another, the State in question wishes to remove from the ICJ's jurisdiction, such as national security, armed conflicts, the conservation, management and exploitation of marine living resources, or the delimitation of land and maritime boundaries).

States that have accepted the Court's jurisdiction are free to supplement, amend or even withdraw their declaration. The same applies to consent given by concluding a treaty containing a compromissory clause, since the States parties to a treaty have the power to withdraw from it in accordance with its terms.

States can also accept the Court's jurisdiction after a dispute has arisen, solely for that particular dispute. Such acceptance can be notified in two different ways.

First, when two or more States differ on a given question, they can agree to submit it to the ICJ and to recognize the Court's jurisdiction to entertain this existing dispute. To that end, they conclude a treaty known as a "special agreement" with the express purpose of submitting their dispute to the Court. Once the special agreement has been notified to it, the Court can entertain the case. It is relatively rare for a dispute to be brought before the Court by special agreement; thus far, such agreements have mainly been used in cases concerning land or maritime boundary delimitations.

Second, if a State has not already recognized the ICJ's jurisdiction when proceedings are instituted against it, it can decide to accept its jurisdiction subsequently so that the Court may entertain the case: when this happens, the Court has jurisdiction by virtue of the *forum prorogatum* rule. This situation is somewhat unusual: to date, there have been only two instances where a State which has not consented in advance to the Court's jurisdiction has agreed to give its consent for the specific purposes of a case (*Certain Criminal Proceedings in France (Republic of the Congo* v. *France)* and *Certain Questions of Mutual Assistance in Criminal Matters (Djibouti* v. *France)*). If such consent is given, the case in question is entered on the Court's docket and takes its normal procedural course. In the absence of such consent, no further action is taken in the case.

The form in which a State's consent is expressed determines the manner in which a case is submitted to the ICJ: when a case is

brought by way of a special agreement, the Court is seised when the Registry is notified of that agreement by either party or by both parties together. In all other instances, the Court is seised through the filing in the Registry of an application instituting proceedings, the document by which an applicant State initiates proceedings against a respondent State before the Court.

Preliminary objections

Respondent States can object to the Court entertaining the dispute submitted to it if they consider that it lacks the power to do so. In that event, they can ask the Court to settle this issue before addressing the merits of the case. They do so by filing preliminary objections, in which they set out the reasons why the Court cannot, in their opinion, rule on the dispute before it. Such reasons may vary, but they usually concern the question whether the Court has jurisdiction, i.e. whether it has the power to settle the dispute at issue. The extent of this power depends, among other things, on the terms of the consent to the Court's jurisdiction given by the States parties to the dispute. Respondent States may argue, for example, that the ICJ lacks jurisdiction to entertain the dispute because it concerns a subject expressly excluded by that State's declaration accepting the compulsory jurisdiction of the Court, or that the conditions set out in the treaty clause conferring jurisdiction on the Court have not been satisfied, since the parties to the dispute did not first attempt to resolve it through negotiation, as they had agreed to do.

States can also raise various other reasons why a case should not be examined on the merits, even if the Court were to have jurisdiction. These might include, for example, the fact that, in the respondent State's view, the Court should not exercise its jurisdiction because the application is inadmissible, since the applicant is not entitled to submit a claim before the Court, since the decision would have no practical effect or would be incompatible with the role of a court, or since the individual whom the applicant State is seeking to protect is not a national of that State or has failed to exhaust the local remedies open to him or her in the respondent State.

Filing preliminary objections has the effect of temporarily preventing the Court from considering the merits of the parties' dispute: the proceedings are suspended to allow the Court to

Name plates of States that have appeared in cases before the Court.

rule on the issues raised by the respondent in its preliminary objections, which must be dealt with as a matter of priority. A separate phase of the proceedings thus opens, which precedes the examination of the merits and during which the Court is called on to settle certain preliminary questions.

In the event of a dispute as to whether the ICJ has jurisdiction, it is for the Court itself to determine its competence; it renders its decision in the form of a judgment, after giving the parties the opportunity to present their arguments, first in writing and then orally during hearings devoted to the preliminary objections. Once the parties have been heard, the Court may decide to uphold a preliminary objection, to reject it or to find that it is not of an exclusively preliminary character and is to be examined subsequently, during the merits phase. Depending on the Court's decision, preliminary objections may have the effect of putting an end to the proceedings or limiting the subject-matter of the dispute in question; if the objections are rejected, however, the proceedings will continue and the Court will address the case on the merits.

Parties to cases before the ICJ frequently avail themselves of the possibility to file preliminary objections, which form an ever-growing part of its work. Over the last decade, preliminary objections have been filed in more than a third of cases brought before the Court.

THE PARTICIPANTS IN THE PROCEEDINGS

The parties

In contentious cases, the Court's function is to settle the legal disputes submitted to it by States. In this regard, it can entertain only disputes between two or more States. Private individuals, international organizations and non-governmental organizations are thus precluded from bringing disputes of any kind before the ICJ.

The Court can entertain a dispute between States only if the States concerned are entitled to participate in proceedings before it. States may acquire this capacity by becoming parties to the Court's Statute, either through membership of the United Nations or by meeting certain conditions laid down by the General Assembly on the recommendation of the Security Council.

In the first instance, United Nations Member States automatically become parties to the Court's Statute when they sign the UN Charter. The Statute is annexed to the Charter and forms an integral part of it. On signing the Charter, Member States also accept the obligations arising under that instrument, including the obligation to comply with the Court's decision in any case to which they may be parties. To date, 193 United Nations Member States have become parties to the Court's Statute in this way and therefore have access to the Court.

The second option concerns States that become parties to the Court's Statute without signing the UN Charter or becoming Members of the United Nations. To do so, they must satisfy conditions fixed by resolution of the General Assembly, including accepting the provisions of the Statute of the Court, complying with the Court's decisions and contributing to its expenses.

Finally, the Court is also open to States which, despite being neither Members of the United Nations nor parties to the Court's Statute, can access the Court provided they meet the conditions set out in a Security Council resolution. Under the terms of that resolution, the Court is open to States that have deposited in its Registry a declaration by which they agree to accept the Court's jurisdiction and comply with its decisions. Declarations may concern a specific dispute that already exists, or disputes or classes of disputes that may arise in the future. Several States have used such declarations to submit a dispute to the Court before becoming Members of the United Nations.

The representatives of the parties before the Court

States have no permanent representatives accredited to the ICJ; their everyday communications with the Court usually take place through their ministry of foreign affairs or their diplomatic mission in the Netherlands. States parties to a case appoint an agent to represent them before the Court for the purposes of a case, either when the proceedings are instituted (through the filing of an application or the notification of a special agreement) or shortly afterwards. States' agents are often their ambassador to the Netherlands or a senior official from their ministry of foreign affairs. Agents must have an address for service at the seat of

The Agents of Costa Rica and Nicaragua in the Certain Activities *and* Construction of a Road *cases.*

The Agent of Ukraine, H.E. Ms Olena Zerkal, during hearings on preliminary objections raised by the Russian Federation.

The Agent of Equatorial Guinea, H.E. Mr. Carmelo Nvono Nca, during hearings on the merits in the Immunities and Criminal Proceedings *case.*

the Court, to which all communications concerning the case are sent; the address is generally that of the State's diplomatic representation accredited to the Netherlands. Agents represent the State that has appointed them before the Court and serve as intermediaries in all exchanges with the Court for the purposes of the case. They receive case-related communications from the Registrar and transmit to the Registrar any correspondence or written pleadings from their appointing State; they are also consulted by the President of the Court on questions relating to the organization of the proceedings in the case in question.

During the oral proceedings, agents open the oral argument of their State and read out its final submissions; they may also deliver part of the State's arguments themselves. Any formal act required of a government is carried out by its agent, who has the power to commit the government before the Court.

Agents are sometimes assisted by a co-agent or deputy-agent. Agents may also receive help from counsel and advocates in preparing written pleadings and delivering oral arguments. States are free to choose their counsel and advocates, who need hold no particular qualifications and may be of any nationality. Since there is no special bar association or professional body whose members are authorized to plead before the Court, one need only have been appointed by a government in order to do so. In the interest of the sound administration of justice, the Court has nonetheless adopted certain directions for use by States appearing before it, inviting them to refrain from designating as agent, counsel or advocate a person who is sitting as judge *ad hoc* in another case before the Court, or any person who has served as a Member of the Court, judge *ad hoc*, Registrar, Deputy-Registrar or higher official of the Court in the three years prior to their appointment.

Parties may thus appoint jurists from their national civil service (in particular, their ministry of justice or ministry of foreign affairs) or recruit external jurists, such as lawyers in private practice or professors of international law. As a result, the teams representing parties before the Court often comprise jurists from various regions and legal traditions, who work (and even plead) in one of the two official languages of the Court, English or French.

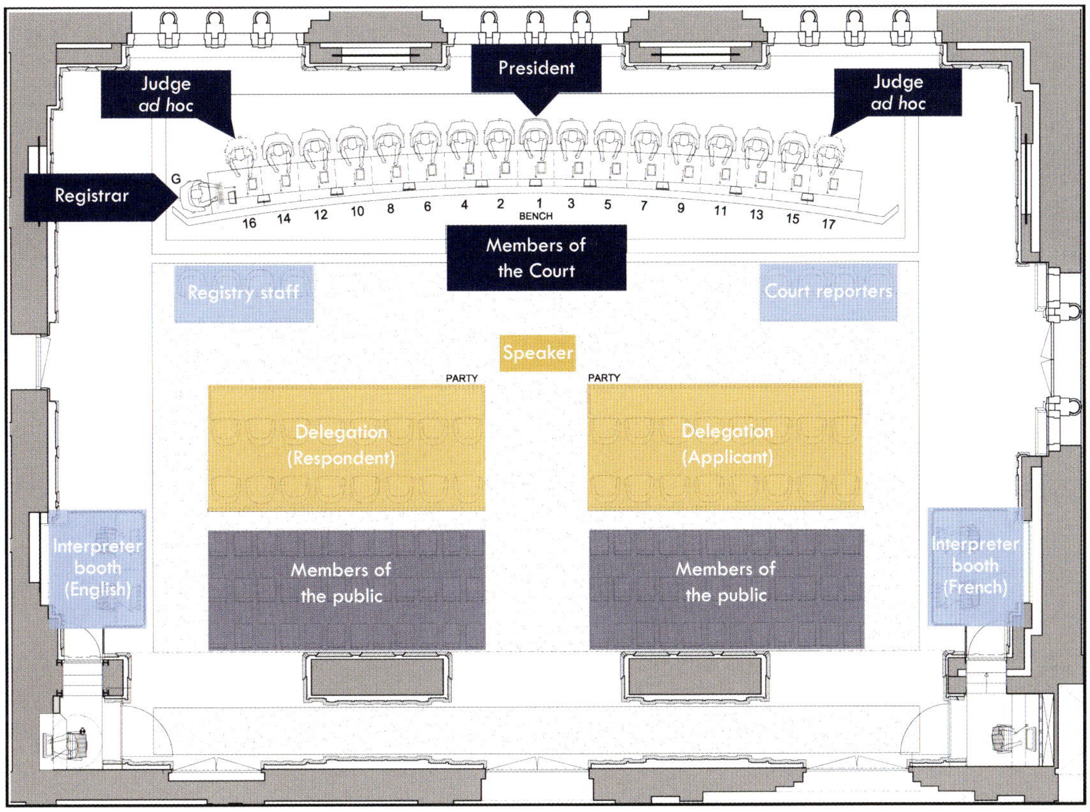

Floorplan of the Great Hall of Justice.

Once designated, agents, counsel and advocates enjoy the privileges and immunities necessary for them to perform their duties independently. Their salaries and fees are borne by the party they represent.

Witnesses and experts

States parties to cases before the Court are free not only to appoint the agents, counsel and advocates authorized to represent them, but also to choose the evidence they wish to produce in support of their respective arguments. In this regard, States may call witnesses and seek an expert opinion from any individual they choose; this has happened in about 15 cases. The parties may file reports prepared by their designated experts during the written proceedings and may request that experts be heard during the oral proceedings.

The Court may also decide, on its own initiative and after hearing the parties, to appoint a person or entity to conduct an investigation or give an expert opinion for the purpose of clarifying a particular point. The Court has exercised this power on just a few occasions in its history, in cases raising factual questions of a technical or scientific nature. In such cases, the Court may be usefully assisted by experts in gathering evidence, establishing in an objective and independent manner the facts relating to the questions before it, and assessing the arguments put forward by the States parties to the case. Recently, the Court has relied on opinions from experts (some appointed by the Court, others by the parties) to establish the starting-point of a maritime boundary, and to determine the existence and extent of environmental damage and assess the amount of the compensation owed as a result.

Third States to proceedings

While most cases before the Court involve only one applicant State and one respondent State, it is nonetheless possible for third States to intervene in ongoing contentious proceedings between other States. Such participation is voluntary and can only be initiated by the third State concerned; neither the Court nor the parties may force a third State to take part in proceedings. Moreover, except in special circumstances, the intervention of a third State does not require the consent of the parties to the case in question.

A State has the right to intervene in a pending case between other States in two situations. First, a third State may intervene if it has a legal interest in the dispute which may be affected by any future decision of the Court. In that event, the State concerned files an application for permission to intervene, generally before the conclusion of the written proceedings in the case. The Court rules on such applications by a judgment in which it decides whether the conditions required for the intervention have been met.

A third State also has the right to intervene in a dispute between other States if that dispute concerns the construction of a convention to which it is a party. It exercises that right by filing a declaration of intervention with the Court, in principle before the opening of the oral proceedings. The Court delivers its decision on the intervention in the form of an order.

In both scenarios, when an intervention is authorized by the Court, the intervening State receives copies of the pleadings and may present its observations both in writing and during the oral proceedings. The consequences for the intervening State depend on the reason for its intervention: if the third State intervenes to present its views on the construction of a convention, the interpretation given in the Court's decision will be binding on it; if it intervenes to protect a legal interest that may be affected by the Court's decision, the State will not, except in special circumstances, be bound by the Court's decision, which is binding only on the parties to the case. The Court has recognized, however, that an intervening State may become a party to the case if it so requests and if there is a valid basis of jurisdiction among all the States concerned. In that situation (which has yet to occur), the Court's decision would also be binding on the intervening State as regards any aspect of the case to which its intervention relates.

A third State which has an interest in ongoing proceedings between other States but does not wish to intervene may ask the Court to provide it with copies of the written pleadings filed in the case. The Court rules on such requests after consulting the parties to the case; as a general rule, it will grant the request if the parties agree and deny it if they object.

Non-State participants

While only States may submit a dispute to the Court, a separate procedure, known as "advisory proceedings", enables certain United Nations organs and duly authorized bodies to request an advisory opinion from the Court on a legal question. Further, any international organization — and any State — that the Court considers likely to be able to furnish information on a question raised in advisory proceedings is given the opportunity to present written or oral statements.

Public international organizations may also present observations before the Court in contentious proceedings, either at the Court's request or on their own initiative.

Public international organizations are international organizations composed of States; it is thus not possible for non-governmental organizations to present observations before the Court in contentious cases, for example by intervening as *amicus curiae*. Any documents communicated to the Court on the initiative of a non-governmental organization in the context of advisory proceedings are not considered as part of the case file but as "publications readily available", which may be consulted at the Peace Palace and referred to by the other participants in the proceedings. •

Agents and counsel during oral proceedings of the Court.

COURT OF

The three Governments agree that for the purpose of
DONE at Bonn on 2 February 1967 in four copies in the
English language.
For the Government of the Kingdom of
Denmark
For the Government of the Federal Republic of
Germany
For the Government of the Kingdom of the
Netherlands

THE COURSE OF THE PROCEEDINGS

What happens when a case concerning a dispute between States is submitted to the Court? These are known as "contentious cases" and they account for the majority of the Court's judicial activity. Advisory proceedings, where an international organ or agency requests a legal opinion from the Court, are covered in a separate chapter.

Institution of contentious proceedings

A dispute between States can be brought before the Court in two ways: either by means of a unilateral application filed by one State against another (which happens in the majority of cases), or through the notification to the Court of a special agreement between States, providing for their dispute to be referred to it.

When proceedings are instituted by an application, the latter indicates the State making it (the applicant) and the State against which the claim is brought (the respondent), the subject of the dispute, the grounds on which the jurisdiction of the Court is based, the precise nature of the claim, and a succinct statement of the facts and legal grounds on which the claim is founded. On receiving the application, the Registrar of the Court transmits a certified copy of it to the respondent.

When proceedings are instituted by means of a special agreement, this must indicate the subject of the dispute and the States that are parties to it. If the notification is not given jointly by the parties, a certified copy of the agreement is sent by the Registrar to any other party to it.

All new cases are then widely publicized: a copy of the application or special agreement notification is sent to the United Nations Secretary-General and to all States to which the Court is open, as well as to any person who requests it. The act instituting proceedings is also published on the Court's website.

The Court usually considers the cases brought before it as a full court. However, the parties can agree to request that a case be heard by a chamber constituted specially for that purpose and composed of at least three judges.

Presentation of arguments

Proceedings before the Court are designed to ensure equality between the parties in the presentation of their arguments. They consist of two phases: one written, the other oral.

Written proceedings

Once the act instituting proceedings has been filed, the Court fixes time-limits for the submission of written pleadings in which the parties set out their arguments. Any evidence cited in support of their claims is normally annexed to these pleadings. Generally speaking, in proceedings instituted by means of an

Special Agreement signed by the Danish, German and Dutch Governments referring the North Sea Continental Shelf *cases to the Court.*

application, the applicant first files a memorial setting out its arguments of fact and law; the respondent then presents its arguments in a counter-memorial.

After the first round of written proceedings is complete, the Court can decide (on its own initiative or at the request of one of the parties) to authorize a second round, for example to enable the parties to respond to any new arguments raised by the opposing party. In most cases, States ask to make use of this possibility.

Written proceedings may be organized differently, however. In some cases, the Court or the parties decide that their pleadings should be submitted simultaneously. In the *Frontier Dispute (Burkina Faso/Niger)* case, for example, each party first filed a memorial, followed by a counter-memorial.

The pleadings remain confidential throughout the written phase and are generally made public on the opening of the oral proceedings.

Oral proceedings

Once the written phase has been concluded, in principle no further documents can be added to the case file by the parties and the case is ready for hearing. During the oral proceedings, the parties' representatives present their arguments to the Court at public hearings, which are normally streamed online. In 2020, in response to the COVID-19 pandemic, the Rules of Court were modified to allow hearings to take place by video link.

The length of time between the end of the written proceedings and the opening of oral proceedings varies according to the Court's schedule, but also on the availability of the parties. Similarly, the duration of the hearings depends on each case. In proceedings instituted by an application, the applicant is heard before the respondent.

In cases brought by means of a special agreement, the parties appear in the order agreed between them or determined by the Court after consulting them.

The oral proceedings are themselves divided into two rounds. During the first round, the parties are asked not to repeat the substance of their written pleadings, but to concentrate on the points that continue to divide them. In the second round, which is generally shorter, the parties are given the opportunity to respond to any new arguments raised during the first round. The parties conclude their presentations by reading out their submissions, i.e. the specific claims on which the Court is asked to rule.

In principle, the parties address the Court in one of its official languages, English or French, and the Registry of the Court ensures that interpretation is provided into the other official language. A full verbatim record of each hearing is then prepared by the Registry, communicated to the parties and published on the Court's website.

Parties can also present evidence during the oral proceedings. A party wishing to call witnesses or experts must provide certain information in advance of the hearings about the witnesses and/or experts and the points their testimony will address. The production of evidence is subject to the authorization of the Court, which decides how witnesses and experts called by the parties will be heard. When it considers it necessary, the Court can also decide to call witnesses or experts of its own accord.

In the case concerning *Application of the Convention on the Prevention and Punishment of the Crime of Genocide (Croatia* v. *Serbia)*, four witnesses and two witness-experts were heard at Croatia's request during two public hearings and one private hearing.

In addition, the hearings provide an opportunity for the Court or its Members to put questions to the parties. The parties are invited to present their responses orally during the hearings or in writing within a time-limit fixed by the Court; each party can then comment on the responses given by the other.

Non-participation in the proceedings

A party may, for any reason, refuse to take part in all (or part) of the proceedings. A party's failure to appear does not prevent the proceedings from taking their course: the written and oral phases take place (with the participation of the applicant), at the end of which the Court delivers its judgment. However, before ruling, the Court must satisfy itself that it has jurisdiction and that the claims are well founded in fact and in law. Failure to appear is relatively rare in practice; to date it has happened about a dozen times.

The Great Hall of Justice set up for hybrid hearings during the COVID-19 pandemic, September 2020.

Deliberation and judgment of the Court

After the hearings, the President declares the oral proceedings closed and the Court retires for deliberation. At the end of this process, which generally takes no longer than six months, the Court delivers its decision in the form of a judgment, which is read out at a public sitting. In response to the COVID-19 pandemic, the Rules of Court were modified to allow such sittings to take place by video link. Once the judgment has been read out, a signed original bearing the seal of the Court is placed in the Court's archives; one is also transmitted to each of the parties. Copies are sent to the United Nations Secretary-General and to all States to which the Court is open, as well as to any person who requests it. The judgment is also published on the Court's website.

A judgment of the Court consists of three parts: (1) the *qualités*, which set out, among other things, the principal procedural steps in the case and the parties' claims; (2) the grounds, which explain the Court's reasoning on the facts and law; and (3) the operative part, which contains the Court's decision. The various paragraphs of a judgment's operative clause are adopted by a majority of the judges present; in the event of a tied vote, the President or presiding judge has the casting vote. The judgment also states whether the English or French text is authoritative. Judges may append a declaration or a separate or dissenting opinion to the judgment to explain their stance on certain points of the decision.

The Court's judgments are final, binding on the parties and without appeal. The Statute of the Court states that a party may, however, make a request to the Court for interpretation of one of its judgments or, in the event of the discovery of a new fact, and subject to certain conditions, an application for revision.

The parties must comply with the Court's judgment. If a party fails to fulfil the obligations incumbent on it under a judgment, the other party can have recourse to the United Nations Security Council, which may, if it deems necessary, make recommendations or decide on measures to be taken to give effect to the judgment.

Proceedings before the Court can take several years. Their duration depends above all on the time taken by the parties to prepare their written pleadings and on any incidental questions that may arise.

Incidental proceedings

The procedural steps in a case are very often subject to change, since various events may occur during the course of the proceedings. There are two main categories of incidental proceedings that can be initiated by the parties: requests for the indication of provisional measures and preliminary objections.

Request for the indication of provisional measures

In some cases, a party will ask the Court to indicate provisional measures. When such a request is made, it is dealt with as a matter of priority by the Court through oral proceedings. The Court then makes an order in which it indicates or refuses to indicate provisional measures.

The principal procedural steps before the Court

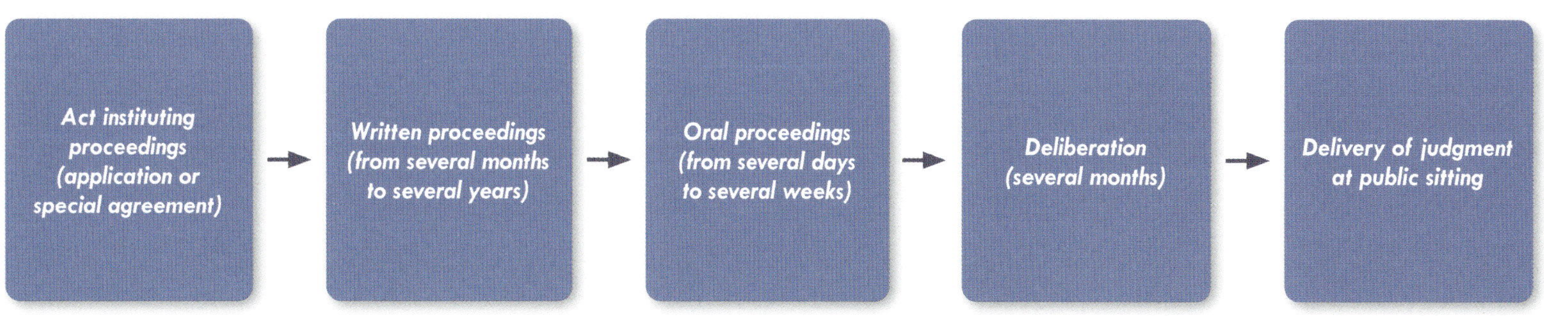

Examination of an expert (centre) by counsel (left and right of centre) during a hearing.

The Agent of New Zealand, Ms Penelope Ridings, at the opening of the hearings in the case concerning Whaling in the Antarctic (Australia v. Japan: New Zealand intervening).

Preliminary objections

A party (usually the respondent) may also challenge the Court's jurisdiction in a case or claim that the Court cannot entertain a case for some other reason. In this instance, the party raises preliminary objections to the jurisdiction of the Court or to the admissibility of the application, and does so even before it has filed its first written pleading. When such preliminary objections are raised, the Court suspends the proceedings on the merits and invites the other party to present a written statement of its observations and submissions on the objections. It then hears the parties during hearings on the objections, before delivering a judgment on them. If the Court finds that it has jurisdiction to entertain a case and that the application is admissible (in whole or in part), or if it decides to delay its decision on these matters until a later stage, the proceedings on the merits are resumed. If the Court finds that it does not have jurisdiction, or that the application is inadmissible, its judgment brings the proceedings to a close.

Other incidental proceedings

Other incidental proceedings include the submission of counter-claims by the respondent, the joinder or discontinuance of proceedings, and requests to intervene by third States.

THE COLLECTIVE DRAFTING OF A DECISION OF THE COURT

The hallmark of the ICJ is undoubtedly its working methods, which are designed, above all, to reflect the collaborative process by which the judges sitting in a case before the Court reach a decision. The way in which the ICJ works, the composition of its Bench and the principle that the Court's jurisdiction is based on State consent are what underpin the characteristic authority and legitimacy attached to Court decisions by the international community. From the earliest days of the Permanent Court of International Justice, which preceded the ICJ, international jurists were convinced that the Court's working methods should reflect its role as a judicial institution of universal character and general jurisdiction. It was thus essential to ensure that the decision taken by the majority of its judges was reflective of a collective deliberation and drafting process, and that all judges were able to participate in that process on an equal basis, since the Court's authority was also dependent on each judge contributing to its judicial work.

The Court therefore decided very early on not to adopt the advocate-general or "judge-rapporteur" system, in which one member is tasked with drafting the majority decision. Instead, a system had to be found that would allow for a truly collective process resulting in an equally collective decision, incorporating each judge's contribution and thereby ensuring the lasting legitimacy of the decision rendered.

But how to reach a collective decision, and how to draft a decision involving 15 judges, or even 17 in cases in which two judges *ad hoc* were chosen? The PCIJ devised a finely tuned system for ensuring that each elected Member and any judges *ad hoc* had an equal opportunity to participate not only in the decision-making, but also in the drafting of the judgment or advisory opinion. This system, which was set out and codified in 1931 by the Resolution concerning the internal judicial practice of the Court, proved successful and was subsequently adopted by the ICJ in 1946. Although it has since been expanded and refined, it is nevertheless fair to say that, in essence, the ICJ's internal practice in 2021 is governed by the same principles and follows the same methods as those established in 1931.

Over time, some aspects of the Court's internal practice have taken on greater or lesser importance. In its early years, for example, the Court made only moderate use of Article 1 of the Resolution concerning its internal judicial practice, which allows the judges to meet after the close of the written proceedings and before the hearings in order to exchange views and identify any points requiring further explanation during the oral phase. Recently, however, it has tended to make more frequent use of this possibility. Such meetings are particularly useful in technical cases in which it is necessary to draw the parties' attention to points that appear to the Court to warrant special attention during the oral proceedings.

The preliminary deliberation ("Article 3 deliberation")

Immediately after the conclusion of the hearings — which may be brief but can sometimes last for several weeks — the Court withdraws to begin its deliberation. To help structure the discussions,

A member of counsel presents their party's arguments to the Court.

Deliberation process as outlined in the Resolution concerning the Internal Judicial Practice of the Court

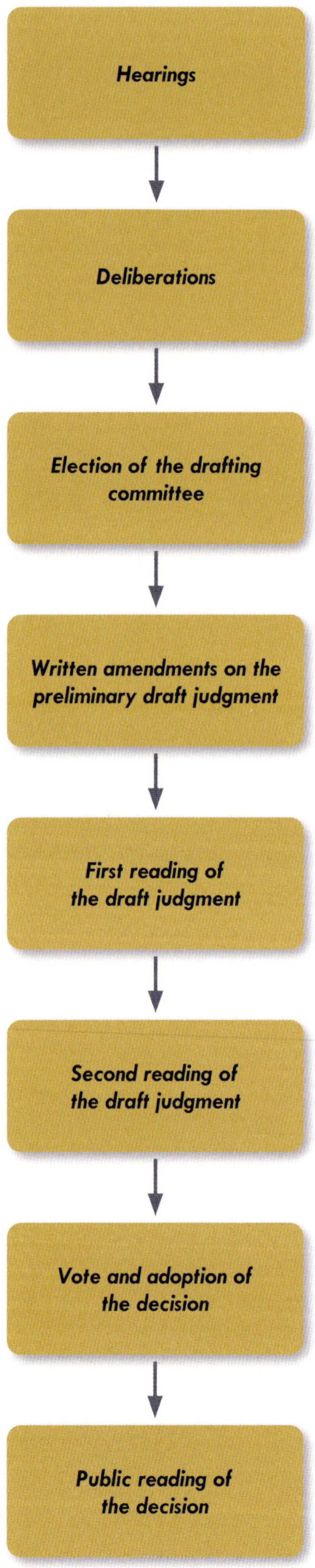

the President prepares a list of issues for consideration; this is a list of points of fact and law which, in the President's view, the Court will need to resolve in its decision. The list enables a systematic approach to be taken to the discussions, although each judge is free to deviate from it, to raise additional questions considered to be relevant and to leave certain questions aside. The preliminary deliberation following the hearings thus does not address how the case should be decided, but simply the questions that it raises. After these initial discussions, the list is amended as necessary and recirculated among the judges, who then prepare their respective "Notes".

Judges' Notes

The judges generally have a few weeks to prepare their written Notes, but this may vary depending on the complexity of the case at hand. In these Notes, each judge expresses his or her tentative opinion on how to resolve the various legal issues raised in the case. This exercise can be described as a solitary one, during which the judges must form and articulate their personal opinions, often in a language that is not their mother tongue. The Notes, which are drafted in either English or French before being translated into the other official language of the Court by the Department of Linguistic Matters, may be extremely detailed or extremely brief, the judges being at liberty to express themselves as they wish. To ensure complete freedom of thought, the judges receive their colleagues' Notes only once they have submitted their own. Notes are strictly confidential and for the judges' use only. They offer the judges an insight into their colleagues' views and an initial idea of the approach favoured by the majority with regard to a particular question. Notes are not binding on their authors, however, who are free to change their opinions, in theory up until the time they cast their vote.

Above, left:
During hearings, a small number of seats are available to the public.

Above, right:
Judge Xue in a meeting with an associate legal officer.

Below, left:
Judges conversing in the Red Room prior to the start of a hearing.

Below, right:
Interpreters provide simultaneous interpretation into French and English during hearings and private meetings of the Court.

The second deliberation ("Article 5 deliberation")

Once the judges have familiarized themselves with the written Notes of their colleagues, a second deliberation is held. Over the course of several sittings, the judges express their opinions orally, in reverse order of seniority, beginning with any judges *ad hoc* and ending with the Vice-President and the President. At the end of each presentation, questions may be asked and discussions ensue with the aim of clarifying the views held by each judge.

It is at this stage that the Court forms its opinion on the points of fact and law that have been raised and on how each legal issue should be resolved. The judges are free to change their opinions, to allow themselves to be persuaded by their colleagues' arguments or, on the contrary, to reaffirm their own views as expressed in their Note. To ensure that the judges are able to express themselves freely and without constraint, these deliberations are strictly confidential; they are therefore not recorded, which is sometimes a shame because from a legal perspective the discussions can be fascinating.

The broad outline of the majority position thus begins to emerge, although usually no vote is yet taken on any point. At the end of this deliberation, which may last for four or five days, the President summarizes the discussions and the majority position. The Court then elects the members of the drafting committee by secret ballot from among those judges whose views coincide with the opinion of the apparent majority. The committee is generally composed of two Members of the Court (sometimes more) and the President, who is a member ex officio, unless he or she does not share the majority opinion, in which case the President is replaced by the Vice-President or by the senior judge if the Vice-President's views also do not align with the majority.

The work of the drafting committee

The first meeting of the drafting committee takes place directly after the deliberation. The purpose of this meeting is to establish the framework of the decision and divide up the work of preparing a preliminary draft judgment in both working languages of the Court, with the assistance of the Registry. The committee's next task is to draft a bilingual text which accurately reflects the opinions expressed by the majority during the deliberations.

The committee generally meets several times prior to the deadline fixed by the Court for the distribution of the preliminary draft: it rephrases, restructures and revises the text until it is satisfied that it has found the best way to formulate the majority's decision in the case and the reasoning followed in reaching that decision.

The preliminary draft, which, like the Notes, is confidential, is then circulated to the judges not sitting on the drafting committee.

Substantive and stylistic written amendments

At this stage, regardless of whether their opinions coincide with those of the majority, the remaining judges are given the opportunity to contribute to the drafting of the decision. Each judge is invited to propose written amendments aimed at improving the committee's preliminary draft. These amendments, which are reviewed by the drafting committee, may concern both style and substance. While some might lead the committee to modify the preliminary draft text, omit entire sections, refine or flesh out the Court's reasoning, or simply improve linguistic consistency between the two language versions, others will be considered incompatible with the majority views and will therefore be rejected.

The drafting committee then updates its text on the basis of the proposed amendments, producing a new version referred to as the draft judgment for first reading.

The first reading

This new draft is then discussed during a first reading by the Court, which takes place in private. The reading may take several days, since the method employed aims to ensure that each sentence and paragraph is examined. A discussion follows, during which some judges may reiterate amendments that had been proposed in writing but were rejected by the drafting committee, providing further explanations as to why they should be adopted. Others may put forward new amendments, critique the structure or overall organization of the text, suggest that a particular sentence be omitted, retained or modified, or even propose that a paragraph be referred back to the committee. The committee may also explain why it rejected certain amendments or used a particular form of words in the reasoning. The work involved in the first reading is both extremely meticulous and comprehensive. Discussions can centre on the position of a comma, but may also address the substantive issue of how the majority's reasoning should be articulated.

In a spirit of collegiality, judges who wish to prepare a separate or dissenting opinion provide the Court with a draft text between the first and second readings. This enables the drafting committee to react and to adjust the text of the decision to take account of their views, if this can be done without misrepresenting the views of the majority. The committee then spends a few weeks preparing its draft judgment before submitting it for second reading.

The second reading

The revised draft judgment is then distributed to the Court in both languages to be examined and adopted with or without modification during the second reading, which is generally shorter than the first. At the end of the second reading, the operative part of the judgment, i.e. the actual decision adopted by the Court in response to the parties' claims, is read out before being put to a vote. Any judge may request a separate vote on a particular point.

Decisions are taken by an absolute majority of the judges present. They vote "yes" or "no" orally on each point and no abstentions are allowed on any of the points on which a vote is taken. Should the votes be equally divided, the President has the deciding vote.

Once this collective process of deliberation, discussion and drafting is complete, each sentence, word and turn of phrase will have been carefully weighed, discussed and agreed, the final decision being the fruit of the concerted efforts of the Court as a whole.

A wax seal is applied to the official copies of the Court's decisions.

The public reading of the decision

In contrast to the practice of international arbitral tribunals, judgments of the Court are delivered publicly at solemn sitting. The delivery takes place at a public session normally held in the Great Hall of Justice in the Peace Palace, during which the President reads out key passages from the judgment, as well as the full text of its operative provisions and the details of the judges' votes. The parties do not know the outcome of the decision in advance; after months of waiting, they listen carefully to what the Court has decided in the case, before receiving their own copies of its judgment.

The Court's decisions are bilingual documents that vary greatly in length (ranging from 10 to 271 pages, to date). The seal of the ICJ is affixed to each copy transmitted to the parties and to the copy placed in the Court's archives.

This, in a nutshell, is how the ICJ organizes its work to ensure that all judges have an equal opportunity to participate in the drafting of its decisions. While each decision of the Court bears the mark of the members of the drafting committee, it is ultimately the work of every judge sitting in the case. Despite the different approaches that might be taken by the judges, owing to their personal character, background, professional experience, or the legal tradition that they represent, the work of the Court demonstrates that those composing it speak a shared language, the language of international law. Bound by a common spirit and conscious that they are representatives of a highly respected institution, the judges of the ICJ are acutely aware of their collective responsibility when called on to render a decision — a decision which is carefully constructed and which aims above all to respond, with the full authority and legitimacy vested in the Court, to the legal questions before it.

Members of the delegations of Croatia and Serbia following the 2015 Judgment in the Genocide case.

WDR

PROVISIONAL MEASURES

When a State party to a dispute considers that there is an imminent risk of irreparable prejudice to its rights, it can ask the Court to indicate provisional measures. These measures are ordered by the judges as a matter of urgency in order to contain the situation until they are able to consider the case on its merits. The aim is to avert any action that might aggravate or extend the dispute before the Court or make it more difficult to resolve.

Who can request provisional measures, and when?

Provisional measures are nearly always requested by the applicant, but they may also be sought by the respondent. For example, in a case brought by Argentina against Uruguay regarding the construction of pulp mills on a river which forms their common boundary, Uruguay (the Respondent) submitted a request for the indication of provisional measures on the grounds that Argentinian citizens who opposed the mill project had blockaded a bridge over the river between the two States' territories and that this action was causing it considerable economic harm.

It should also be noted that the Court has the power to indicate provisional measures on its own initiative, without being asked to do so by one of the parties to the dispute. That said, although the Court has recalled that it has this power in several of its orders, it has yet to make use of it in practice.

Requests can be made at any time during the proceedings. While they are often made when the application instituting proceedings is filed, they can also be submitted later. For instance, in proceedings instituted by Nicaragua against Costa Rica for "violations of [its] sovereignty and major environmental damages on its territory", Nicaragua did not request provisional measures until two years after the case was brought before the Court. It all depends on the situation and how it develops.

Urgent proceedings

When a request for the indication of provisional measures is submitted, it is a matter of urgency. There is an alleged need to prevent the situation from worsening and to avoid irreparable prejudice being caused to the rights of the State concerned before the case is decided on the merits.

As a first step, the President may write to the parties and ask them to refrain from doing anything that might prevent a decision of the Court to indicate provisional measures from having its appropriate effects.

In any event, the request is considered to have priority; it takes precedence over all other cases, and consideration of the request is scheduled without delay. If the Court is not sitting when the request is submitted, it is convened at once.

To save time, the request is examined in expedited proceedings, which generally take place in oral form only. This allows the judges to give a ruling very quickly. They usually deliver their decision within an average of three to four weeks, but it is possible for

Members of the Court in the Bol Room of the Peace Palace.

them to move even faster. In the *LaGrand* case *(Germany* v. *United States of America)*, in which a person was due to be executed the day after the Court was seised, it gave its decision within a mere 24 hours.

However quickly it deals with the request, the Court delivers its ruling in the form of an order read out by the President at public sitting.

Under what conditions can the Court indicate provisional measures?

Provisional measures must not be taken lightly. The Court must act quickly to protect the rights of the requesting State, but without impairing the rights of the other party. A fair balance must be struck. The Court therefore assures itself that a number of conditions are met:

- Since its jurisdiction is not compulsory, the Court determines whether it has prima facie jurisdiction, i.e. whether the provisions relied on by the applicant appear, on the face of them, to constitute a basis on which its jurisdiction in the case could be founded.

- It also examines whether the rights which the applicant claims on the merits are at least plausible (given the need to act swiftly, the Court does not at this stage have the time to determine whether they actually exist).

- It ascertains whether a link exists between the substantive rights to be protected and the measures requested.

- It considers whether there is a risk of irreparable prejudice to those rights.

- Lastly, the Court determines whether there is urgency, i.e. whether the risk of irreparable prejudice is real and imminent (this condition is met where the acts liable to cause such prejudice can "occur at any moment" before the Court makes a final decision in the case).

If any one of these conditions fails to be satisfied, the Court will reject the request for provisional measures, which has happened in about half of all instances since the Court was founded. However, this does not prevent either party from submitting a fresh request, if the situation changes.

On the other hand, if all the above conditions are met, the Court will indicate provisional measures. Two options are possible:

- The Court can of course indicate the measures requested.
- It may also order other measures.

In practice, the measures indicated are extremely varied. Ranging from an obligation not to execute an individual to those aimed at preventing certain serious acts (such as acts of discrimination or genocide), they have included requirements to refrain from any dredging and to fill in a trench dug on disputed territory, to demilitarize a particular area, to keep documents under seal, or to take effective measures to prevent the destruction and ensure the preservation of certain evidence. It all depends on the circumstances of the case, of course.

What effects do provisional measures have?

An order indicating provisional measures has binding effect; in other words, the measures in question must be implemented by the parties concerned (as the Court made clear in its celebrated 2001 Judgment in the *LaGrand* case). The order thus creates obligations for the party or parties to which it is addressed. If a party fails to comply with these obligations, its international responsibility is engaged.

Compliance with the measures indicated is crucial. There are several reasons for this, the first being the need to protect the rights of the parties in dispute. Indeed, several years may pass between the institution of proceedings and delivery of the final decision. It may thus be necessary for the Court to take steps to prevent any act that might aggravate or extend the dispute submitted to it, or make it more difficult to resolve. Beyond the rights of the parties, compliance safeguards the very function of the Court.

Above:
Members of the delegations of Cambodia and Thailand at the opening of hearings on provisional measures.

Below:
Sketch-map of the provisional demilitarized zone identified by the Court in its 2011 provisional measures Order.

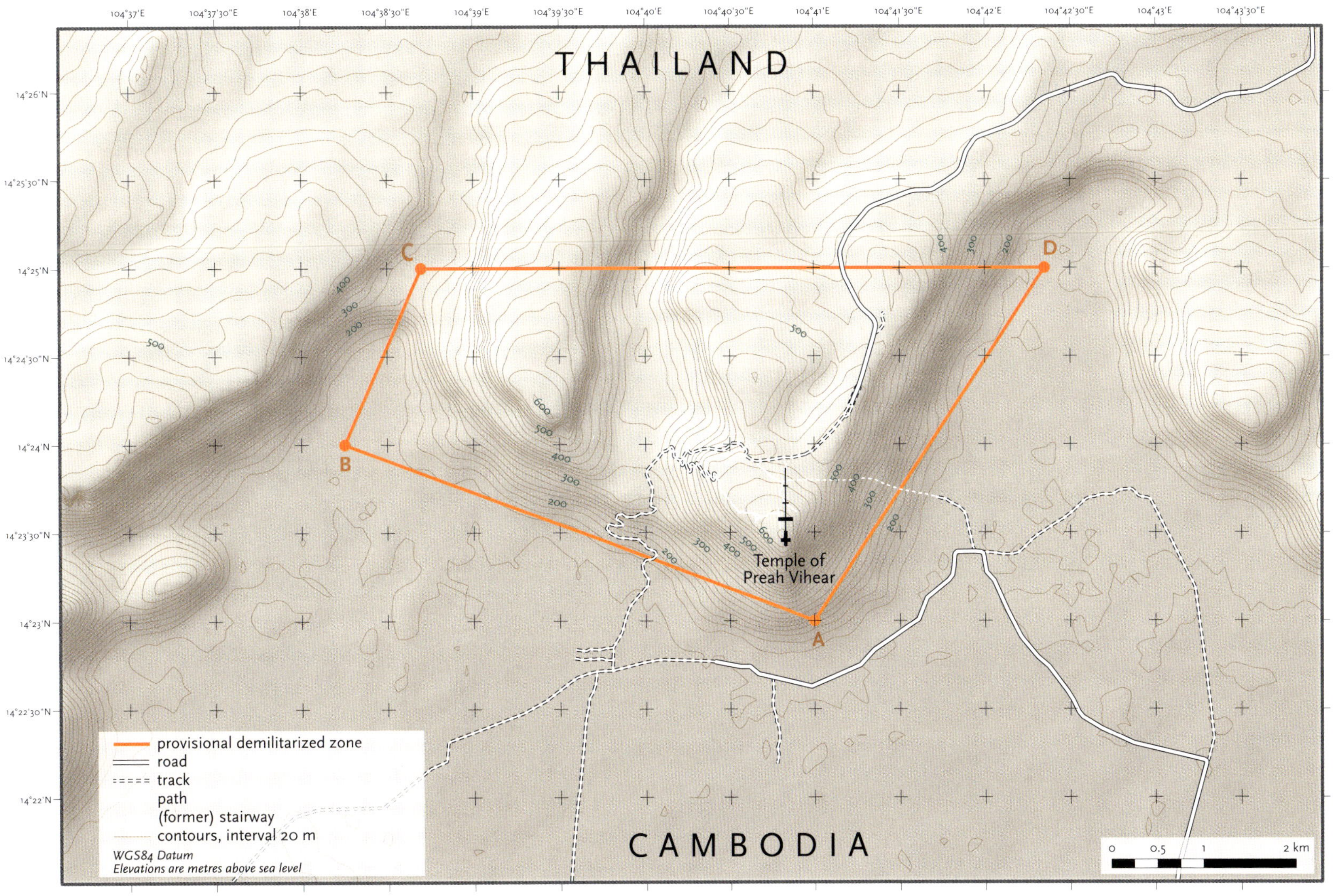
THAILAND
CAMBODIA
Temple of Preah Vihear
A
B
C
D
provisional demilitarized zone
road
track
path
(former) stairway
contours, interval 20 m
WGS84 Datum
Elevations are metres above sea level
0 0.5 1 2 km

Number of cases in which provisional measures were requested, per decade

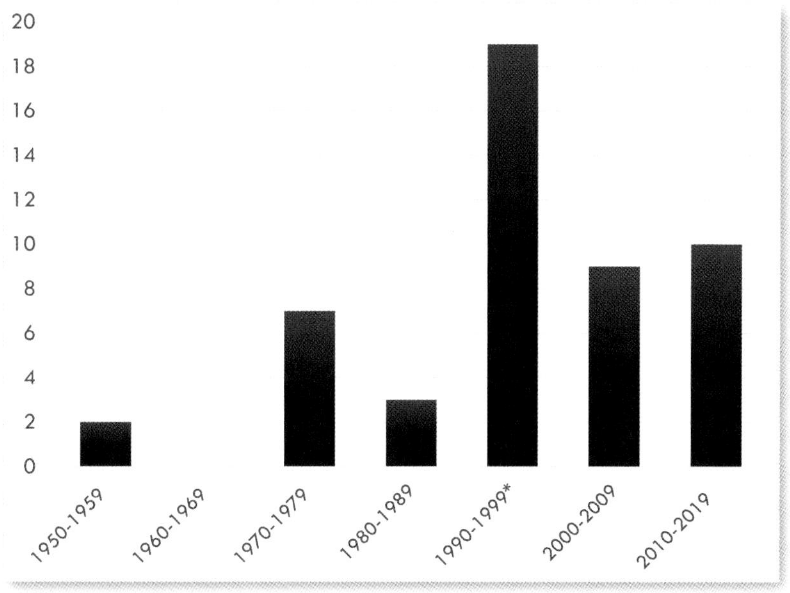

* *Includes the ten cases on the* Legality of Use of Force, *in which the applicant submitted requests for the indication of provisional measures in each case.*

It is essential for a court to have the time it needs to examine a case calmly and to render its decision, without fear of it being deprived of effect before it is even delivered.

The States to which provisional measures are addressed must be in a position to report to the judges on how they are fulfilling their obligations. The Court often seeks information from States on the implementation of the measures required of them and, to this end, directs them to submit periodic reports.

To strengthen its monitoring of the implementation of provisional measures, the Court recently introduced an actual oversight mechanism, which provides for the establishment of an *ad hoc* committee, composed of three judges, to assist it in this area. In practice, the committee examines the information provided by the parties, reports periodically to the Court, and recommends potential options for it. Any decision, if required, is taken by the Court.

Given that they are ordered pending a final judgment in the case, provisional measures are indicated on an interim basis only. They may thus be modified in the course of the proceedings if the situation so requires. Hence in a case in which the judges directed Australia, whose agents had seized documents from the office of a legal adviser to Timor-Leste, to keep the documents under seal in order to protect and safeguard their confidentiality, the Court authorized Australia several months later to return the documents to the adviser in question.

In any event, the raison d'être for provisional measures disappears once the final decision is delivered. For example, in a case between Equatorial Guinea and France, the Court ordered France to grant the premises claimed to be occupied by Equatorial Guinea's diplomatic mission in Paris the protection afforded by the Vienna Convention on Diplomatic Relations (i.e. to ensure their inviolability, prevent any intrusion or search, etc.). Since the Court, in its Judgment on the merits of the case, ultimately found that these premises never acquired the status of premises of the diplomatic mission within the meaning of the Convention, the Order ceased to produce any effect and France is no longer obliged to grant such protection to the building in question.

Finally, it is important to bear in mind that the decision by which the Court indicates provisional measures in no way prejudges the question of its jurisdiction to entertain the merits of the case (it may happen that the Court indicates provisional measures but later finds that it lacks jurisdiction), or any question relating to the admissibility of the application or to the merits themselves. An order on provisional measures does not affect the right of the States parties to a dispute to make their case on these points.

In practice, in the vast majority of instances, provisional measures are implemented by the States concerned, and governments have always complied with the obligation to submit reports on the implementation of such measures. It must be said that this gives them an opportunity to emphasize and explain that they are fulfilling their obligations. There are numerous examples of provisional measures being effectively implemented by the States to which they were addressed:

- In connection with its interpretation of the Court's 1962 Judgment in the *Temple of Preah Vihear* case between Cambodia and Thailand, the Court created a provisional demilitarized zone, delimited according to precise co-ordinates, and directed both countries to withdraw from that area. A few days after the Order was made, the Court was informed that markers had been placed on the ground to demarcate the zone.
- In the case concerning *Immunities and Criminal Proceedings (Equatorial Guinea* v. *France)*, France took no measures that

conflicted with the Court's Order directing it to provide the alleged premises of Equatorial Guinea's diplomatic mission in Paris with the protection afforded by the Vienna Convention.

- More recently, Pakistan stayed the execution of an Indian national who had been sentenced to death.

Increasing importance

Provisional measures are now in very frequent use. States appear to see them as an essential tool to protect their rights. The criteria set by the Court are clear and well established, and States are thus aware of the conditions under which their request may be granted. Consequently, the number of provisional measures proceedings has increased significantly: while a mere 22 requests were submitted to the Court between 1945 and 1998, 35 were made between 1999 and 2020. In the last ten years, moreover, provisional measures have been requested in a third of all cases brought before the Court.

The Agents of India and Pakistan during hearings on provisional measures in the Jadhav case.

Voting Started
Item 88 Draft resolution A/73/L.84/Rev.1
5/22/2019
12:56:09 PM
AFGHANISTAN
ALBANIA
ALGERIA
ANDORRA
ANGOLA
ANTIGUA-BARBUDA
ARGENTINA
ARMENIA
AUSTRALIA
AUSTRIA
AZERBAIJAN
BAHAMAS
BAHRAIN
BANGLADESH
BARBADOS
BELARUS
BELGIUM
BELIZE
BENIN
BHUTAN
BOLIVIA (PLURINATI...
BOSNIA-HERZEGOVINA
CHAD
CHILE
CHINA
COLOMBIA
COMOROS
CONGO
COSTA RICA
COTE D'IVOIRE
CROATIA
CUBA
CYPRUS
CZECH REPUBLIC
DEM PR OF KOREA
DEM REP OF THE CO...
DENMARK
DJIBOUTI
DOMINICA
DOMINICAN REP...
ECUADOR
EGYPT
EL SALVADOR
EQUATORIAL GUINEA
ERITREA
ESTONIA
ESWATINI
ETHIOPIA
FIJI
FINLAND
FRANCE
GABON
GAMBIA
GEORGIA
GERMANY
GHANA
GREECE
GRENADA
GUATEMALA
GUINEA
GUINEA-BISSAU
GUYANA
HAITI
HONDURAS
HUNGARY
ICELAND
INDIA
INDONESIA
IRAN (ISLAMIC REPU...
IRAQ
IRELAND
ISRAEL
ITALY
JAMAICA
JAPAN
JORDAN
KAZAKHSTAN
KENYA
KIRIBATI
KUWAIT
KYRGYZSTAN
LAO PDR
LATVIA
LEBANON
LESOTHO
LIBERIA
LIBYA
LIECHTENSTEIN
116
AGAINST:6
ABSTENTION:56

THE DEVELOPMENT OF THE COURT'S ADVISORY FUNCTION

In addition to its function of settling disputes between States, the Court has another equally important function: to render advisory opinions at the request of United Nations organs and specialized agencies. An advisory opinion seeks to answer a question of international law that is of interest to the organ or body raising it. For example, the institution concerned may need an answer to the question in order to carry out its functions. In other cases, tension may have surfaced among Member States of the United Nations about a sensitive issue, and the request for an advisory opinion can be an attempt to bring some clarity on that issue from an authoritative judicial institution.

Article 96 of the UN Charter gives the General Assembly and the Security Council the power to request an advisory opinion from the Court on any legal question. The General Assembly may also authorize other organs of the United Nations, specialized agencies or related organizations to ask the Court for advisory opinions on legal questions "arising within the scope of their activities". At present, two other UN organs, one subsidiary organ of the General Assembly, one related organization and 15 specialized agencies are authorized to submit such requests.

Advisory opinions are presented in a similar way to judgments of the Court. They include a summary of the proceedings, the Court's reasoning and the operative provisions. Judges may attach declarations and separate or dissenting opinions to them. Like judgments, advisory opinions are delivered at a public sitting of the Court and read out by the President.

The status and legal force of advisory opinions differ significantly from those of judgments of the Court. An important difference is that while judgments are binding on the parties to a case, advisory opinions are not binding, even on those States that participate in the proceedings. Another key difference is the purpose of advisory opinions: they answer a question put to the Court by another UN organ or body and do not settle a dispute between States, as is the case with judgments. In this sense, the outcome of advisory proceedings concerns not just two States but the international community as a whole. Finally, advisory proceedings are less frequent than contentious proceedings: while the Court has handled over 150 different contentious cases in its 75-year history, it has delivered only 27 advisory opinions.

The subjects covered in advisory opinions

Requests for advisory opinions fall roughly into five different categories.

First, several requests have been made for the Court to clarify institutional issues relating to the functioning of the United Nations. These opinions, which were among the first handed down by the Court, related to such issues as conditions for membership in the United Nations, whether the United Nations can bring a claim for damages following the death of a person in the service of the Organization, the effect of decisions of the United Nations Administrative Tribunal ordering compensation,

On 22 May 2019, the General Assembly adopted a resolution on the Court's Advisory Opinion on the Legal Consequences of the Separation of the Chagos Archipelago from Mauritius in 1965*, by recorded vote (116 in favour, 6 against and 56 abstentions).*

United Nations bodies entitled to request an advisory opinion

United Nations organs

- General Assembly
- Security Council
- Economic and Social Council
- Trusteeship Council

Subsidiary organ of the General Assembly

- Interim Committee of the General Assembly

Specialized agencies and related organization

- International Labour Organization
- Food and Agriculture Organization of the United Nations
- United Nations Educational, Scientific and Cultural Organization
- World Health Organization
- International Bank for Reconstruction and Development
- International Finance Corporation
- International Development Association
- International Monetary Fund
- International Civil Aviation Organization
- International Telecommunication Union
- International Fund for Agricultural Development
- World Meteorological Organization
- International Maritime Organization
- World Intellectual Property Organization
- United Nations Industrial Development Organization
- International Atomic Energy Agency

and whether peacekeeping operations should be financed by the general budget of the United Nations.

Second, the Court has delivered advisory opinions on important questions of treaty interpretation. In particular, it has addressed difficult questions concerning the effect of reservations made by States when ratifying the Genocide Convention; in other words, the Court considered what would be the effect of a declaration made by a State, when ratifying the Convention, stating that it does not consider certain provisions of the Convention applicable to it. It has also answered questions of interpretation concerning the constituent instruments of specialized international organizations and agreements between international organizations and States.

Third, a number of advisory opinions have dealt with the international status of territories, including South West Africa, Western Sahara and the Chagos Archipelago. It is worth noting that various questions surrounding the status and administration of South West Africa account for no fewer than four of the 27 advisory opinions given by the Court.

Fourth, a request for an advisory opinion may relate to certain aspects of an existing dispute. For example, in one advisory opinion, the Court was asked whether Western Sahara at the time of colonization by Spain was a territory belonging to no one *(terra nullius)*; this question was also of relevance in a dispute between Spain, Morocco and Mauritania. In its advisory opinion, the Court provided an answer to that particular question, which was submitted to it by the General Assembly of the United Nations pursuant to Article 96 of the Charter of the United Nations. However, the Court's opinion was not intended to — and did not — settle the dispute pending between the States concerned. An advisory opinion should not have the effect of circumventing the fundamental principle of consent by a State to the judicial settlement of its dispute with another State, a principle repeatedly reaffirmed in the Court's jurisprudence.

Fifth, the Court has been called upon to deal in its advisory opinions with important issues in international relations, such as whether the construction of a wall in the occupied Palestinian territory complied with international law, and whether the unilateral declaration of independence in respect of Kosovo was in conformity with international law. These opinions, which are some of the most recent given by the Court, have attracted great interest around the world.

In certain circumstances, advisory opinions may become binding on the basis of specific treaties, statutes or provisions contained in the constituent instrument of international organizations.

Bodies that have requested an advisory opinion (by number of opinions requested)

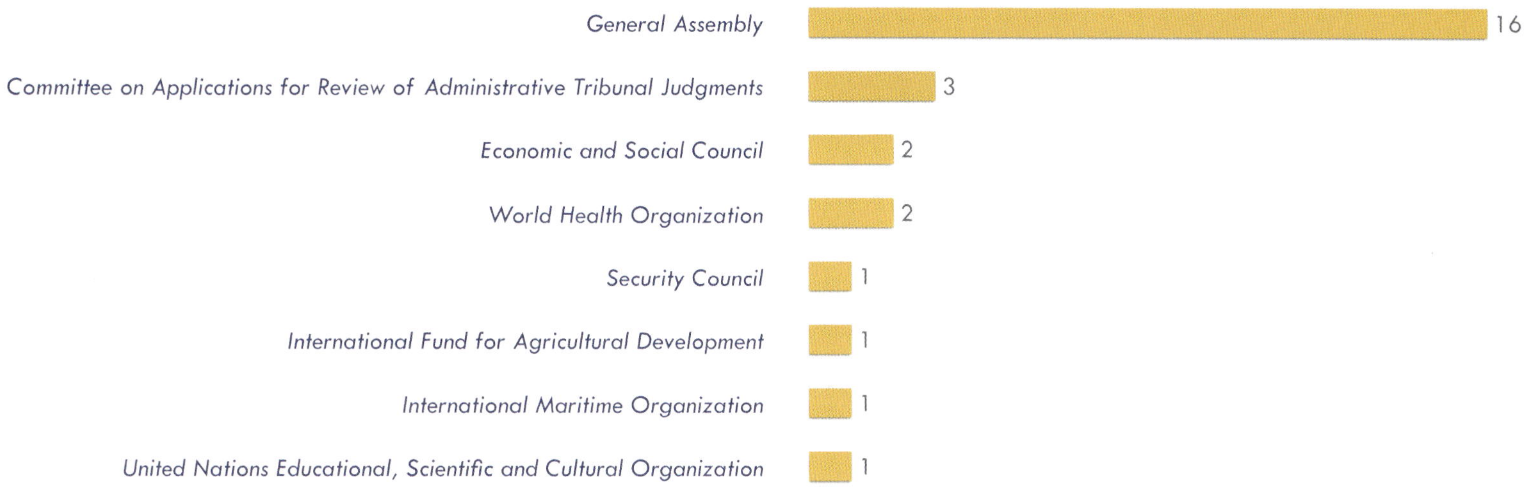

For instance, the Court may be asked to give an advisory opinion regarding decisions of international administrative tribunals such as the Administrative Tribunal of the International Labour Organization and the United Nations Administrative Tribunal (from 1955 until 1995). Likewise, the Court may be called upon to give an opinion which will settle a dispute between a State and an international organization and be considered binding between them, pursuant to the provisions of a specific treaty. Such a mechanism is provided for in the Convention on the Privileges and Immunities of the United Nations, for example. As an illustration, the Court dealt on that basis with a dispute between the United Nations and Malaysia relating to the question of whether a Special Rapporteur of the Commission on Human Rights was immune from legal process before national courts.

The life cycle of an advisory opinion

Advisory proceedings begin with the filing of a written request, which is communicated to the Court by the body authorized to do so in accordance with the UN Charter. The Registrar then immediately informs all States entitled to appear before the Court and gives them an opportunity to submit written statements relating to the question. In addition, any international organizations likely to be able to furnish information on the question are also notified of the request and given an opportunity to submit statements. States and organizations having submitted statements are given the opportunity to provide further comments on the statements made.

The written proceedings are generally shorter than in contentious proceedings between States; in case of urgency, they may even not take place. In the practice of the Court, written statements have varied both in number and length. For example, the Court received written statements from almost 30 States in the *Nuclear Weapons* advisory proceedings and close to 35 States in the *Wall* advisory proceedings, while in other instances, the Court has received statements from about ten States.

All States and organizations having received invitations to give written statements are then invited to make an oral statement at public sittings held on dates fixed by the Court, whether or not they have participated in the written phase. The oral proceedings normally last a few days but may exceptionally run for several weeks. For example, in the *Legal Consequences for States of the Continued Presence of South Africa in Namibia* case, 24 sittings took place over a period of more than a month. After the closing of the oral proceedings, the preparation of the Court's opinion follows the same deliberation and drafting process as judgments. Like judgments, advisory proceedings are also concluded by the delivery of the opinion at a public sitting of the Court.

The importance of advisory opinions

While the number of judgments in contentious cases far exceeds that of advisory opinions, and only judgments in contentious cases are binding on the parties pursuant to the Court's Statute and Rules, the impact of the Court's advisory opinions should not be underestimated. Indeed, the legal questions submitted

States having participated in advisory proceedings

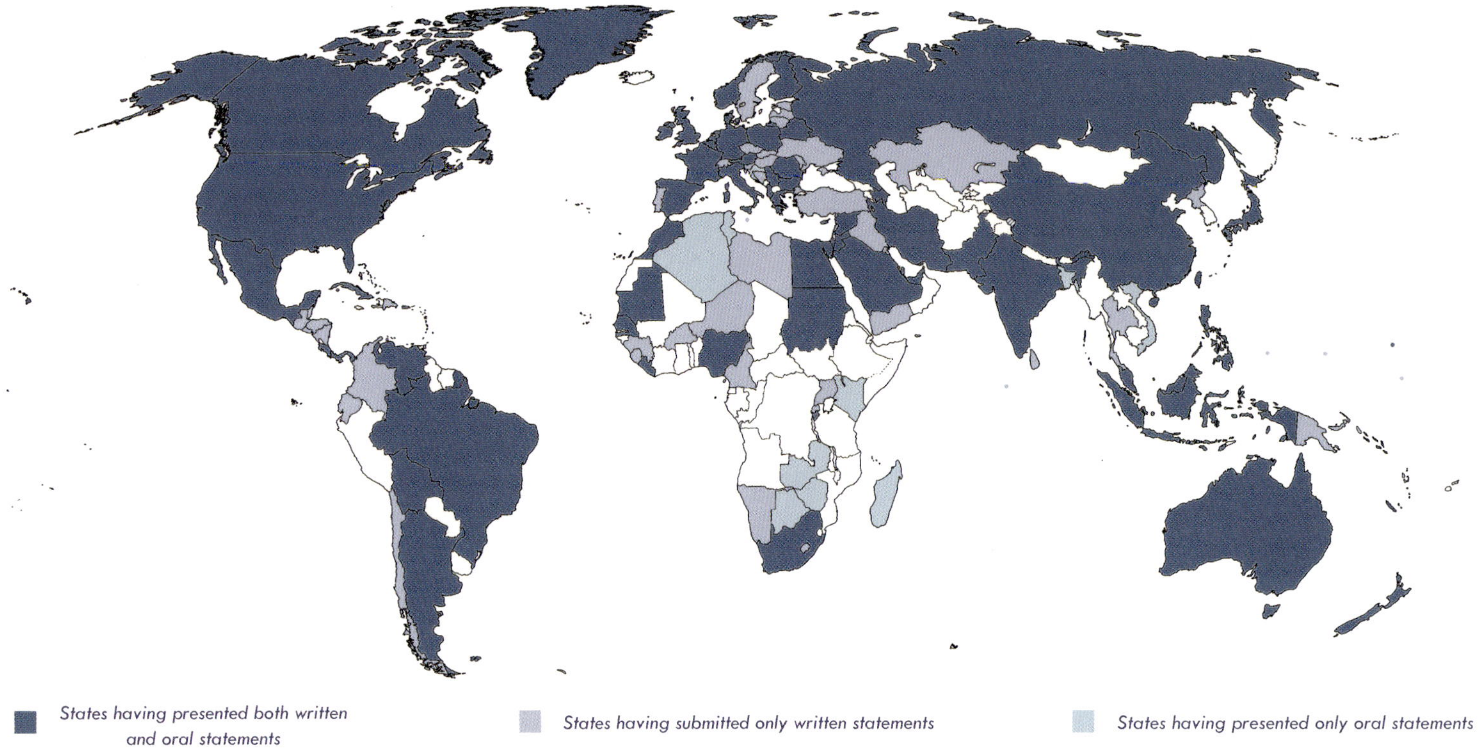

to the Court in the context of advisory proceedings may be of interest for the entire international community. Often, advisory proceedings will attract a large amount of media attention and press coverage. It is no exaggeration to say that, when the Court considers a major question of international law in an advisory opinion, the world's attention turns to The Hague.

Some of the best known advisory opinions include the Court's 1996 opinion on the legality of the threat or use of nuclear weapons, its 2004 opinion on the legal consequences of a wall in the occupied Palestinian territory, its 2010 opinion on the accordance with international law of the unilateral declaration of independence in respect of Kosovo, and its 2019 opinion on the legal consequences of the separation of the Chagos Archipelago from Mauritius in 1965. But other advisory opinions, perhaps less known to the public, have also played a key role in shaping international law. For example, in the Court's 1951 opinion on *Reservations to the Convention on the Prevention and Punishment of the Crime of Genocide*, the Court addressed key questions on the functioning of multilateral treaty relations which remain relevant to this day. The same could be said of the Court's advisory opinions on the status of South West Africa, which laid down fundamental rules of international law concerning the status of international territories. Then there were the multiple opinions which helped clarify and develop the institutional law of the United Nations, such as the Court's two early advisory opinions on the admission of new Member States to the United Nations, its 1948 opinion clarifying that the United Nations had international legal capacity, and its 1954 opinion where the Court made it clear that the judgments of the United Nations Administrative Tribunal were binding on the United Nations. Indeed, as the international community has developed, the advisory procedure of the Court has proven an important tool for answering pressing questions facing the international community.

Journalists in the press room during the reading by President Shi of the Advisory Opinion in the Legal Consequences of the Construction of a Wall in the Occupied Palestinian Territory case.

Journalists from around the world gathered in the Great Hall of Justice.

THE ICJ AND THE PROTECTION OF HUMAN RIGHTS

As the principal judicial organ of the United Nations, the ICJ helps the Organization fulfil its purposes, as set out in the Charter, which include maintaining international peace and security and achieving international co-operation in promoting and encouraging respect for human rights and fundamental freedoms for all without distinction. The Court contributes to the achievement of these objectives in keeping with its mission, which is to settle, in accordance with international law, disputes submitted to it by States and to respond to requests for advisory opinions from authorized United Nations organs and specialized agencies.

A contentious jurisdiction limited to inter-State disputes

In exercising its contentious jurisdiction, the Court can only entertain disputes between States, since they alone may bring a case before it. In this regard, the Court differs from the international criminal courts and tribunals founded more recently to try individuals for acts constituting international crimes (such as genocide, crimes against humanity and war crimes). Examples of these include the International Criminal Tribunal for the former Yugoslavia (ICTY) and the International Criminal Tribunal for Rwanda (ICTR), both *ad hoc* courts created by the United Nations Security Council, and the International Criminal Court (ICC), the first permanent international criminal court, established by the Rome Statute of 1998. Unlike these institutions, the ICJ does not have jurisdiction to try individuals since it is not a criminal court, nor does it have a prosecutor who can initiate proceedings. Nevertheless, it is possible for the same situation — an armed conflict, for example — to give rise to separate proceedings before the ICJ and a criminal court or tribunal, each institution operating within its own area of competence. For instance, the conflicts that devastated the territories of the former Socialist Federal Republic of Yugoslavia in the 1990s led both to the creation of the ICTY, before which several individuals were prosecuted and tried for crimes committed during those conflicts, and to the institution of a number of inter-State proceedings before the ICJ concerning the responsibility of certain States for violations of the Convention on the Prevention and Punishment of the Crime of Genocide.

The ICJ is also different from judicial bodies that examine alleged violations of human rights treaties applicable between States of a given region, such as the European Court of Human Rights (Strasbourg, France), the Inter-American Court of Human Rights (San José, Costa Rica) and the African Court on Human and Peoples' Rights (Arusha, Tanzania). These three courts can consider applications from private individuals and entertain disputes between individuals and States, which is not permitted under the ICJ's Statute.

Although individuals cannot appear as parties before the ICJ, the Court has nevertheless ruled on questions concerning the protection of human rights in its decisions. Through its general jurisdiction, the Court can in fact entertain any question of international law — including those concerning the protection of human rights — which has enabled it to contribute, in its own way, to the development of international law in this area.

Reading of the Judgment in the Obligation to Prosecute or Extradite *case in the Japanese Room of the Peace Palace.*

The Court played its part as this area of international law gradually developed after the adoption of a series of — largely multilateral — instruments, for the most part under the auspices of the United Nations: the 1948 Universal Declaration of Human Rights was followed by the 1966 International Covenants on Civil and Political Rights and on Economic, Social and Cultural Rights, as well as a series of instruments prohibiting and punishing specific acts and practices (torture, genocide, racial discrimination, slavery and forced disappearances), protecting specific categories of persons (women, children, refugees, stateless persons, migrant workers or those with a disability) or safeguarding through regional human rights treaties certain rights in Member States of a particular region.

While some of these instruments provide for a dispute regarding their interpretation or application to be submitted to the Court, most also establish an independent organ responsible for monitoring the application of their provisions by States parties. Examples of such organs include the Human Rights Committee and the Committee on the Elimination of Racial Discrimination, which oversee the application of the International Covenant on Civil and Political Rights and the Convention on the Elimination of All Forms of Racial Discrimination, respectively. The ICJ's jurisdiction in the area of human rights thus runs parallel and is complementary to that of these specialized organs; the Court has also on occasion made reference to the observations and conclusions of such organs in its decisions.

An evolving role

In its early years, the Court above all touched on questions of human rights incidentally, when considering disputes concerning matters of general international law, or treaties or conventions addressing other or related areas. For instance, in the *Barcelona Traction* case, Belgium relied on its right of diplomatic protection to seek compensation for the damage caused to its nationals (as shareholders in the Barcelona Traction, Light and Power Company, a Canadian company) as the result of actions taken against that company in Spain. In principle, the right of diplomatic protection belongs to the national State of the (natural or legal) person that allegedly suffered harm resulting from a violation of international law (in the *Barcelona Traction* case, Canada). When examining the question whether Belgium could act on behalf of its nationals in this case, the Court observed that, in international law, some obligations are binding on States, not only in relation to another State but towards the international community as a whole ("obligations *erga omnes*"). As examples of such obligations, the Court referred to those deriving in particular from the prohibition of genocide and from the principles and rules concerning the basic rights of the human person, including protection from slavery and racial discrimination. The Court was of the opinion that, given the importance of the rights in question, all States could be considered to have a legal interest in their protection.

As the *Barcelona Traction* case shows, the Court has thus been required to address the rights of private individuals in cases concerning diplomatic protection, the mechanism by which a State, acting on behalf of a natural or legal person that is one of its nationals, brings before the Court another State accused of causing damage to that person in breach of international law. In exercising its right of diplomatic protection, a State thus takes up the case of one of its nationals by instituting international proceedings against the State allegedly responsible for the damage suffered by the person concerned.

It is thus possible for a State to exercise its right of diplomatic protection in order to assert the internationally guaranteed human rights of one of its nationals. For example, in its 2010 Judgment in the *Ahmadou Sadio Diallo* case between Guinea and the Democratic Republic of the Congo (DRC), which concerned the treatment in the DRC of Mr. Diallo, a Guinean national, the Court ruled that the measures taken by the DRC to arrest, detain and expel Mr. Diallo violated certain provisions of the International Covenant on Civil and Political Rights and the African Charter on Human and Peoples' Rights, and that the DRC was thus under an obligation to make reparation to Guinea, in the form of compensation, for the injury suffered by Mr. Diallo.

Reading of the Judgment on the question of compensation in the Diallo *case in the auditorium of the Hague Academy of International Law.*

RÉPUBLIQUE DE GUINÉE

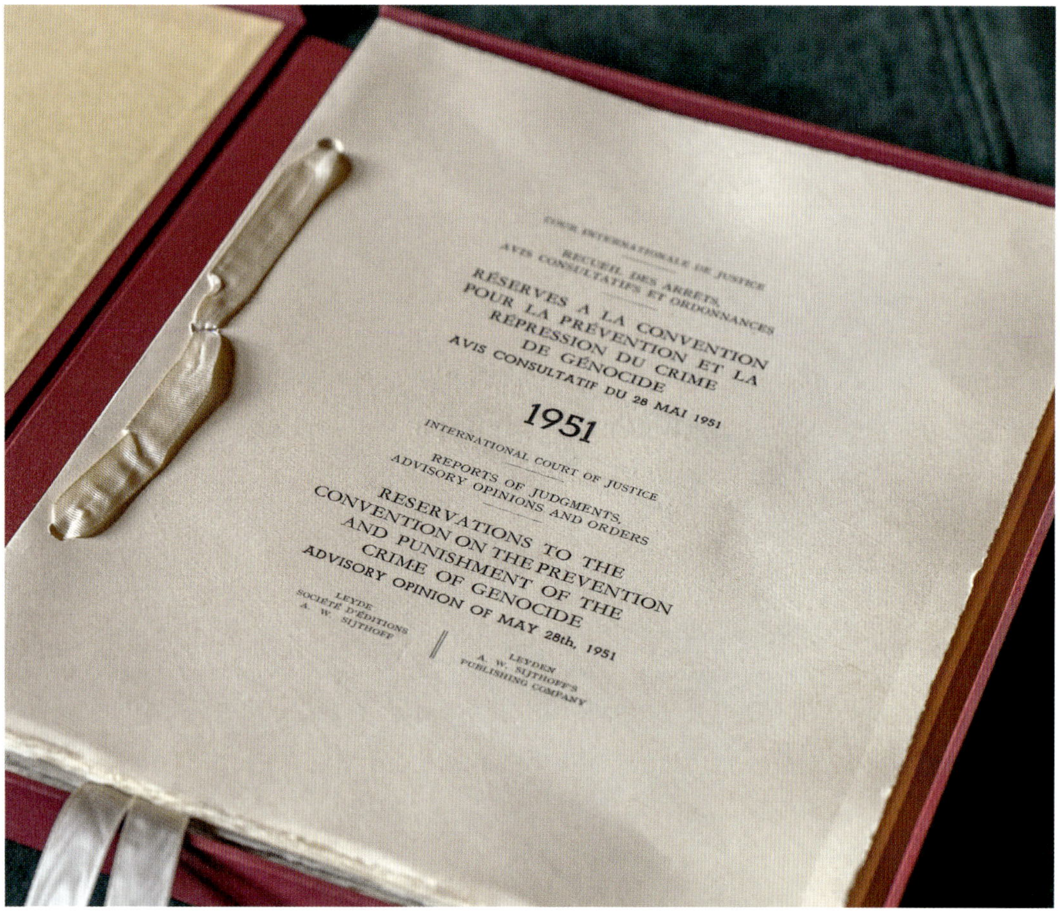

The Court's 1951 opinion on reservations to the Genocide Convention addressed key questions on the functioning of multilateral treaty relations.

The Court has also ruled on situations in which the rights of a State and its nationals are interdependent, notably in cases involving the 1963 Vienna Convention on Consular Relations, which requires States parties to inform the consular authorities of another State without delay when a national of that State is arrested or detained, and to inform the person concerned without delay of his or her right to communicate with the consular post of his or her country. For example, the Court interpreted and applied the provisions of this Convention in the *LaGrand* case, brought by Germany against the United States following the arrest, detention and sentencing to death of two German nationals, brothers Karl and Walter LaGrand. On 3 March 1999, the day after the proceedings were instituted, and the day set for the execution of Walter LaGrand, the Court made an Order indicating provisional measures, in which it directed the United States to take all measures at its disposal to ensure that Walter LaGrand was not executed pending the final decision of the Court in the proceedings. In its final decision on the merits, delivered in 2001, the Court concluded that by not informing the LaGrand brothers of their consular rights without delay following their arrest, and by thereby depriving Germany of the possibility to provide consular assistance in a timely fashion, the United States had breached its obligations to Germany and its nationals under the Convention. In its Judgment, the Court also expressly stated that its Orders indicating provisional measures have binding force. Questions of consular rights were also addressed by the Court in the cases concerning *Avena and Other Mexican Nationals (Mexico* v. *United States of America)* and *Jadhav (India* v. *Pakistan)*; in its Judgments in those cases, it directed the respondent States to provide review and reconsideration of the convictions and sentences of the foreign nationals concerned.

Invoking diplomatic protection is subject to certain conditions, including "the prior exhaustion of local remedies": a State can exercise its diplomatic protection only if its national has exhausted all available remedies in the State said to be responsible for the injury caused. There are, however, a few exceptions to the requirement that local remedies must first have been exhausted, notably when no remedy or no effective remedy exists.

Since the end of the 1990s, the Court has increasingly been seised of disputes concerning alleged violations of human rights under instruments that specifically oblige States parties to respect and protect those rights. For instance, the Court has over the years been called to rule on the interpretation and application of treaties relating to the prevention and punishment of the crime of genocide, the prohibition of torture and other cruel, inhuman or degrading treatment or punishment, the elimination of racial discrimination, and the protection of civil and political rights and of economic, social and cultural rights. The Court has also heard cases relating to several of the major conflicts, upheavals or humanitarian crises to have afflicted the second half of the twentieth century, such as the armed conflicts in the African Great Lakes region and on the territories of the former Yugoslavia, and the situation in the occupied Palestinian territory.

A significant contribution

Through its contentious and advisory proceedings, the Court has influenced the development of international human rights law by interpreting its rules and principles and clarifying its scope and status. For example, it has recognized that certain norms, such as the prohibition of torture and genocide, are of such importance for the international community that they must be upheld at all times. Regarding genocide more specifically, the Court has observed that the obligation to prevent genocide under the Convention on the Prevention and Punishment of the Crime of Genocide requires States that are aware, or that should normally have been aware, of a serious danger of acts of genocide being committed to employ all means reasonably available to them to prevent its occurrence. The Court has also stated that this obligation has no territorial limit and applies to any State wherever it may be acting or may be able to act. In other cases, the Court has focused on the consequences deriving from a situation in which a territory is occupied by a State, and has confirmed that the occupying State has an obligation to ensure respect for the applicable rules of international human rights law and international humanitarian law in the occupied territory. As regards decolonization, the Court has noted on multiple occasions that respecting the right to self-determination is an obligation *erga omnes* — owed by States to the international community as a whole — and that all States have a legal interest in protecting that right.

Through its judgments, advisory opinions and orders, the Court is thus able not only to contribute to the development of international human rights law, but also to play a decisive and concrete role in ensuring respect for the human rights of individuals and populations residing in the States that appear before it.

Uruguay

THE ICJ AND THE PRESERVATION OF THE ENVIRONMENT

The emergence of questions of environmental protection on the ICJ's docket is a somewhat recent occurrence, reflecting the international community's increasing awareness of the potentially harmful effects of human activity on the natural world. Indeed, the protection and preservation of the environment first became a matter of concern for the United Nations in the 1960s, when the General Assembly decided to convene an international conference that would provide guidelines "to protect and improve the human environment and to remedy and prevent its impairment". This novel initiative culminated in the adoption of the 1972 Stockholm Declaration, which laid the groundwork for the development of environmental law as a separate field of public international law.

In 1992, a second United Nations conference on the environment took place in Rio de Janeiro, Brazil. Commonly known as the Earth Summit, it was the largest gathering of world leaders of its time, bringing together Heads of State and representatives from 179 countries and resulting in several treaties and declarations aimed at protecting the environment, including the Convention on Biological Diversity, the Framework Convention on Climate Change and the United Nations Convention to Combat Desertification.

Over the years, growing concerns about the environment have led to additional international treaties containing obligations to protect it, as well as provisions enabling the Court to settle disputes arising in this regard. As a result, the Court has been seised of an increasing number of disputes involving obligations under environmental law, such as those relating to the protection of shared or common resources, the preservation of the marine environment, the protection of international watercourses and the conservation of biological diversity and protected wetlands.

The ICJ has contributed to the development of environmental law in various ways. Through its jurisprudence, the Court has gradually recognized that all States have an interest in protecting the environment as a common concern of humankind and has clarified key rules and principles applicable to this area of international law.

In the *Corfu Channel* case between Albania and the United Kingdom, the very first case to come before the ICJ, the Court laid the groundwork for one of the central tenets of environmental law: the "no harm" principle. In recognizing in its 1949 Judgment that every State has an obligation "not to allow knowingly its territory to be used for acts contrary to the rights of other States", the Court made a statement of principle which came to have a major impact on the formation of environmental law. Some 20 years later, this idea would find expression in Principle 21 of the Stockholm Declaration (and later Principle 2 of the Rio Declaration), whereby States have "the responsibility to ensure that activities within their jurisdiction or control do not cause damage to the environment of other States or of areas beyond the limits of national jurisdiction". In its early days, however, the Court was primarily concerned with bilateral relations between States and their sovereign spheres; the notion of the environment as an independent legal concept had yet to emerge.

The delegation of Uruguay in discussion during hearings in the Pulp Mills *case.*

> *The Court . . . recognizes that the environment is not an abstraction but represents the living space, the quality of life and the very health of human beings, including generations unborn.*
>
> Legality of the Threat or Use of Nuclear Weapons

> *This need to reconcile economic development with protection of the environment is aptly expressed in the concept of sustainable development.*
>
> Gabčíkovo-Nagymaros Project (Hungary/Slovakia)

The environment as a legal interest to be protected

The question of the need to protect the environment as an independent legal interest would not come before the Court until several decades later. In 1973, just one year after the Stockholm Declaration, the Court faced its first environmental dispute in the two *Nuclear Tests* cases. The Applicants, New Zealand and Australia, argued that the atmospheric nuclear tests conducted by France in the South Pacific Ocean violated international law. They contended that the radioactive fallout from these tests posed a threat not only to the life, health and well-being of their people, but also to the environment and the biosphere as such. Although the Court ultimately dismissed the two Applications on the ground that France had put an end to the dispute by making a unilateral undertaking to cease its atmospheric nuclear tests in the Pacific Ocean, this was not before it had issued an Order indicating provisional measures to prevent irreparable harm to the environment and human life caused by further tests. For the first time in its history, the Court recognized the environment as a legal interest to be protected as such. Some 20 years later, New Zealand tried to reopen the case, arguing that France had failed to comply with its international obligations by conducting underground nuclear tests. While the Court did not uphold New Zealand's request, it did expressly recognize that States have an obligation to respect and protect the natural environment.

From that point onwards, environmental protection entered the mainstream of ICJ jurisprudence. In its 1996 opinion on the *Legality of the Threat or Use of Nuclear Weapons*, the Court recognized that the environment is under daily threat and that nuclear weapons could have catastrophic environmental consequences. It relied specifically on its Judgment in the *Corfu Channel* case to support the idea that all States have an obligation to ensure that activities within their jurisdiction or control do not cause damage to the environment.

The next crucial step in weaving environmental protection into the broader fabric of public international law was taken by the Court in 1997, with its Judgment in the case concerning the *Gabčíkovo-Nagymaros Project*. In this case, the Court was asked to settle a dispute between Slovakia and Hungary arising from the termination of a large project along the Danube, Europe's second-longest river, which forms part of their shared boundary. In 1977, the Governments of Hungary and Czechoslovakia (Slovakia's predecessor) had signed a treaty by which they agreed to an ambitious project that involved constructing a barrage system, two hydroelectric power plants and water-management facilities along the Danube, and deepening the riverbed. The project came under intense criticism for its environmental impact on the river, however, and the Hungarian Government decided to suspend it in 1989, acknowledging that it lacked adequate knowledge of the project's environmental, seismological and ecological risks. In 1992, Hungary terminated the 1977 Treaty and abandoned the project altogether on environmental grounds. The Government of Czechoslovakia (and from 1993, that of Slovakia) nevertheless proceeded with the project, unilaterally diverting the flow of the Danube on its territory on the basis of a provisional solution that did not require Hungary's co-operation. Following intense diplomatic exchanges, the States submitted their dispute to the Court by way of a special agreement.

In its pleadings, Hungary argued that the project would have a serious impact on the water quality of the Danube and would condemn the river's flora and fauna and their natural habitats to extinction. In Hungary's view, this amounted to a "state of ecological necessity", which justified the suspension and termination of the 1977 Treaty. Although the Court rejected Hungary's "ecological necessity" plea given the high degree of uncertainty surrounding the environmental risks posed by the project, it nonetheless made some important contributions to international environmental law through its Judgment in this case.

First, it recognized that because environmental damage is often irreversible, all States have a general duty of vigilance to prevent it from occurring. This duty suggests that States must

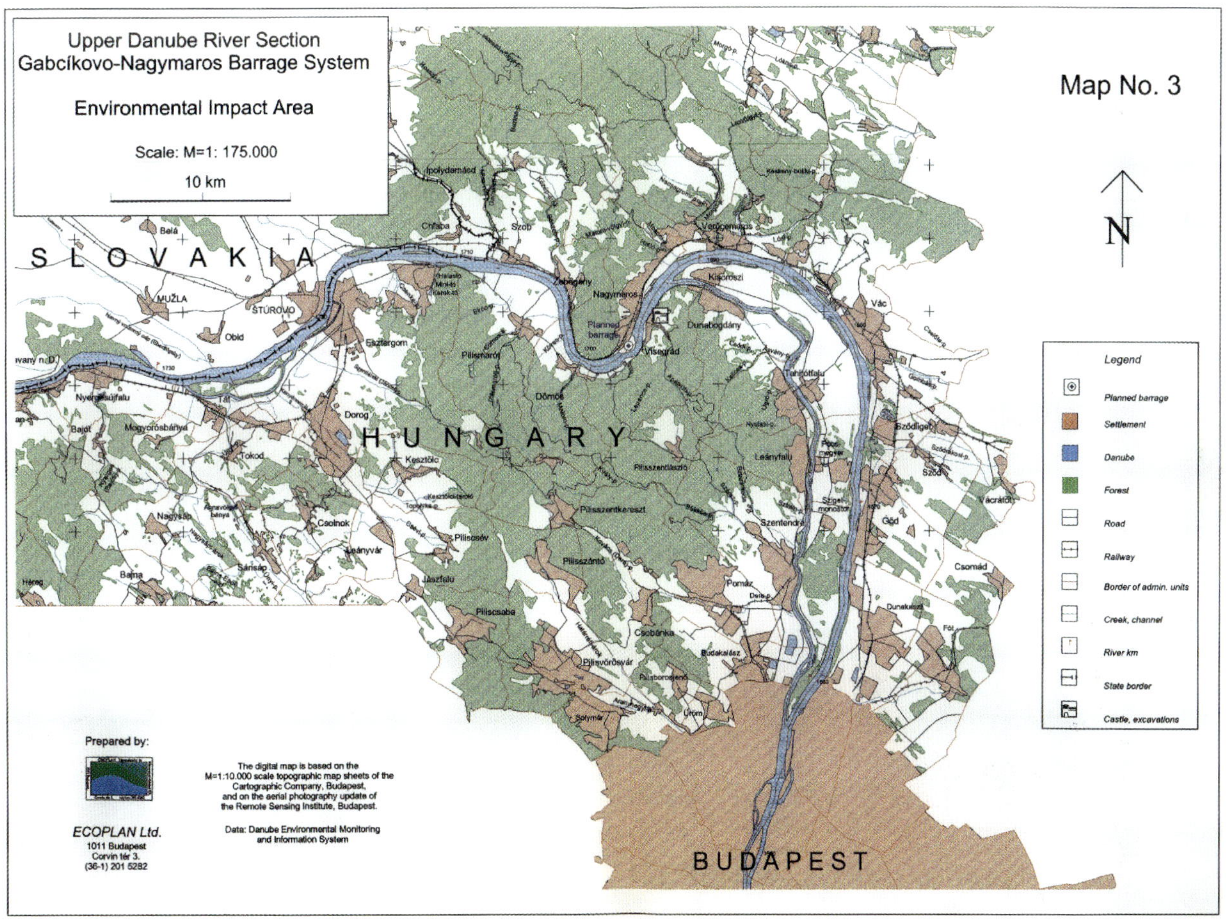

Environmental impact area of the Gabčíkovo-Nagymaros Project (Štúrovo to Budapest), Memorial of Hungary.

Photographs depicting environmental damage in the area of the San Juan River, Memorial of Costa Rica on compensation.

exercise due diligence when undertaking projects that might affect the environment. The Court also stressed that States are under a continuous obligation to ensure the sustainability of the development of economic and industrial activities. They must therefore take into account and give proper weight to environmental standards not only when they contemplate new activities, but also when they pursue activities begun in the past. In the Court's view, environmental protection must go hand in hand with economic development and must be given consideration when interpreting and applying other rules of international law. It is in this context that the Court referred for the first time to the "concept of sustainable development", reflecting "the need to reconcile economic development with protection of the environment".

States' obligations relating to environmental protection

The Court further articulated its understanding of international environmental law in the case concerning *Pulp Mills on the River Uruguay*, in which it acknowledged that States engaging in activities that may adversely affect the environment of another State are subject to certain procedural obligations. The Applicant, Argentina, argued that Uruguay's unilateral construction of two pulp mills on the River Uruguay would have serious consequences on the river's aquatic environment and was in breach of several obligations under the international treaty governing the river's rational utilization. In its 2010 Judgment, the Court reaffirmed that sustainable development requires reconciling riparian States' right to economic development with the continued conservation of the river, and stated that it is only through co-operation that States can manage environmental risks and prevent environmental damage. The Court took the view that States must therefore comply not only with substantive obligations of due diligence, but also with certain procedural obligations of environmental risk management. The Court found that by authorizing the construction of the pulp mills without giving Argentina any prior notification, Uruguay had breached its obligation to allow Argentina to assess the environmental risks of the proposed plans and suggest possible changes. It further observed that the obligation to conduct an environmental impact assessment where there is a risk that an industrial activity may have significant transboundary effects on the environment is so prevalent in international practice that it forms part of general international law.

The Court built on these findings in its 2015 Judgment on the merits in the joined cases concerning *Certain Activities Carried Out by Nicaragua in the Border Area (Costa Rica* v. *Nicaragua)* and the *Construction of a Road in Costa Rica along the San Juan River*

(Nicaragua v. *Costa Rica)*. In its decision, the Court further clarified the obligation of States to carry out an environmental impact assessment before embarking on an activity that has the potential to adversely affect the environment of another State. By recognizing procedural obligations as part of general international law, the ICJ has helped enhance environmental protection.

Reparations for environmental damage

Another way in which the Court has significantly contributed to the preservation of the environment is in determining appropriate remedies in instances where environmental damage has been established. Before 2018, the Court addressed environmental concerns mainly from the perspective of prevention and risk management, and had yet to examine the consequences flowing from environmental damage or whether States have a duty of reparation. In 2018, however, the Court had occasion to address these questions in its Judgment in the case concerning *Certain Activities Carried Out by Nicaragua in the Border Area*. In the merits phase, the Court found that Nicaragua had violated Costa Rica's sovereignty by excavating three *caños* (channels) and establishing a military encampment in the area between the San Juan River and the Caribbean Sea, part of which was designated as protected wetlands of international importance under the 1971 Ramsar Convention. It further found that Nicaragua's conduct had impacted some 6.19 hectares of vegetation and destroyed about 300 trees. Costa Rica claimed compensation for a number of losses, including timber, biodiversity, air quality and erosion control.

In its decision, the Court recognized that international law requires compensation for damage to the environment. This includes compensation not only for the expenses incurred by Costa Rica to restore the wetlands to their prior condition, but also for the impairment of environmental goods and services. In assessing environmental damage, the Court considered the ecosystem as a whole, rather than attributing values to specific categories of environmental goods and services. Relying on equitable considerations, the Court stressed that the absence of scientific certainty as to the extent of environmental damage does not preclude compensation, which should approximately reflect the value of the damage. The Court ultimately awarded US$120,000 for the impairment or loss of environmental goods and services, US$2,708 for the restoration costs incurred by Costa Rica, and US$236,032 for the costs and expenses incurred by Costa Rica as a direct consequence of Nicaragua's unlawful activities on Costa Rican territory.

Within the limits of its judicial function, the ICJ has made substantial contributions to international environmental protection. In *Legality of the Threat or Use of Nuclear Weapons*, it recognized that "the environment is not an abstraction but represents the living space, the quality of life and the very health of human beings, including generations unborn". In the *Gabčíkovo-Nagymaros Project*, it further noted that respect for the environment concerns not only States, but "the whole of mankind". By recognizing the environment as an independent legal concept and integrating its protection into the corpus of general international law, the Court has clarified environmental obligations and helped protect the environment for present and future generations.

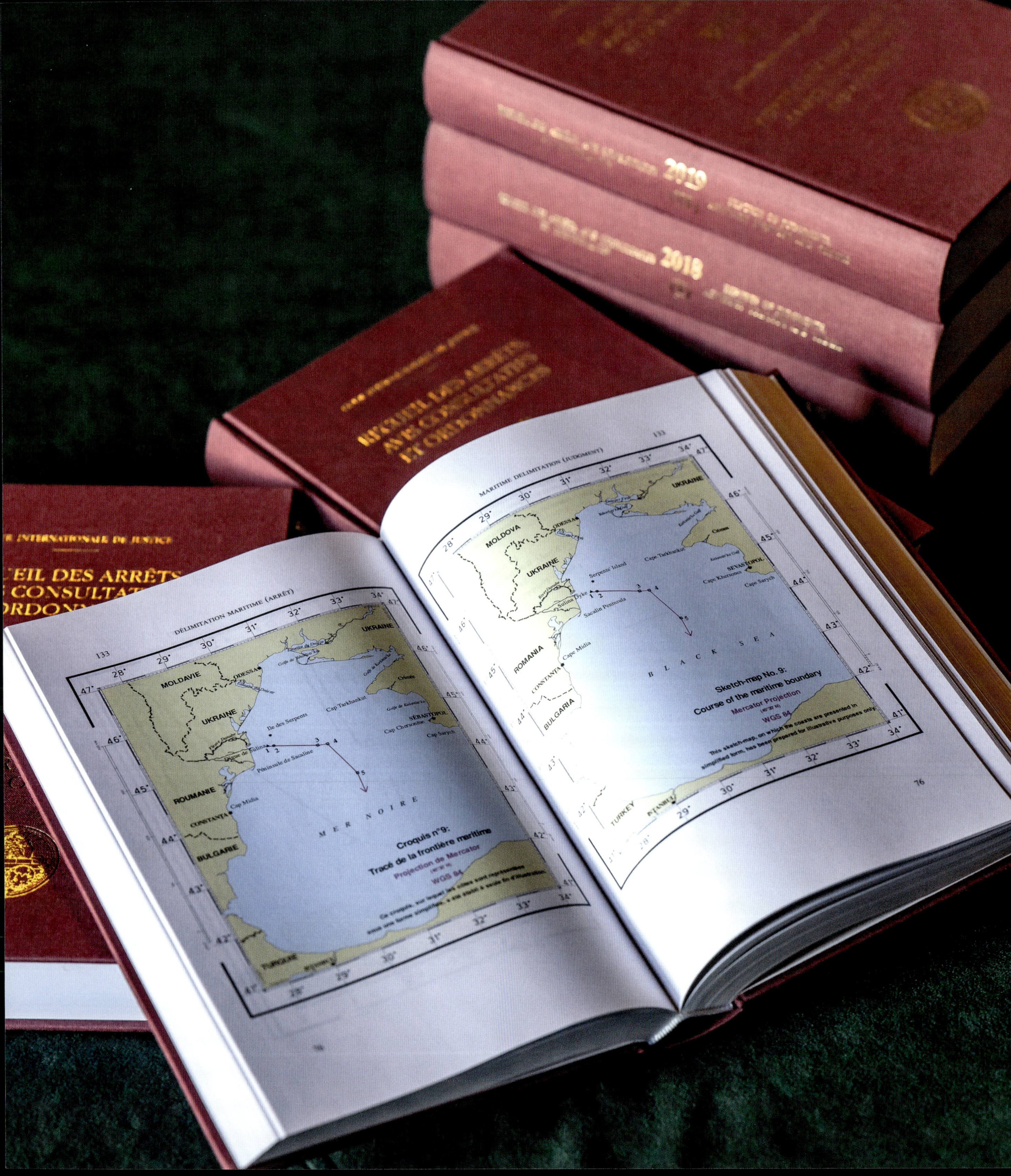

2019
2018
RECUEIL DES ARRÊTS,
EIL DES ARRÊTS
DÉLIMITATION MARITIME (ARRÊT)
133
MOLDAVIE
ODESSA
UKRAINE
Ile des Serpents
Cap Tarkhankut
Crimée
SÉBASTOPOL
Cap Chersonèse
Cap Sarych
Péninsule de Sacaline
ROUMANIE
Cap Midia
CONSTANTA
BULGARIE
TURQUIE
M E R N O I R E
Croquis n°9:
Tracé de la frontière maritime
Projection de Mercator
WGS 84
MARITIME DELIMITATION (JUDGMENT)
133
MOLDOVA
ODESSA
UKRAINE
Serpents' Island
Cape Tarkhankut
Crimea
SEVASTOPOL
Cape Khersones
Cape Sarych
Sulina Dyke
Sacalin Peninsula
ROMANIA
Cape Midia
CONSTANTA
BULGARIA
TURKEY
B L A C K S E A
Sketch-map No. 9:
Course of the maritime boundary
Mercator Projection
WGS 84
This sketch-map, on which the coasts are presented in simplified form, has been prepared for illustrative purposes only.
76

THE ICJ AND TERRITORIAL AND MARITIME DISPUTES

The Court is regularly seised of disputes concerning land or maritime delimitations: since its inception, almost a third of the contentious cases on its docket have concerned or concern such matters.

Generally speaking, it is only after attempting to settle their disagreement by diplomatic means, and following the failure of negotiations, that States opt to submit their territorial or maritime disputes for resolution by arbitral or judicial means; in practice, the mechanism often chosen is the Court. The political and strategic importance of boundary demarcation probably explains why most boundary disputes (17 out of 31) have been brought before the ICJ by special agreement. These instruments allow States to agree on the precise task entrusted to the Court in the resolution of their dispute.

Cases concerning boundary delimitations, whether instituted by special agreement or by unilateral application, have been brought before the Court by States from all regions of the world. In settling such disputes, the Court seeks to foster stable international relations in the regions concerned, and at the same time to contribute to the development of international delimitation law.

The delimitation of land boundaries

In its decisions concerning territorial delimitation, the Court has been able to clarify the various elements required to establish a State's sovereignty over a given territory and to identify certain principles applicable in these matters.

The task of the Court, when called on to settle a dispute of this type, is essentially to determine which party has produced the more convincing evidence that it has sovereign rights over the territory at issue.

To this end, the Court first determines whether an established boundary already exists (making sure that it has not been modified by express or tacit international agreement). In so doing, it looks first and foremost for a territorial title, i.e. a document with legal force for the purpose of establishing territorial rights on the basis of which the dispute might be resolved, for example a treaty between neighbouring States fixing their shared boundary. When such a title is relied on by a party, the Court may be required to interpret its terms in order to clarify certain provisions, or even to determine its scope and whether it is applicable in the case before it.

When a territorial dispute cannot be fully or partially resolved on the basis of a territorial title, either because no such title exists or because it is insufficient or unclear, the Court examines whether sovereignty can be established using the *effectivités* (i.e. evidence demonstrating the exercise of authority by one or other of the parties over the territory in question) presented in support of the territorial claim. In practice, *effectivités* may take the form of various acts and activities (such as legislative or regulatory

The course of the maritime boundary between Romania and Ukraine in the Black Sea as delimited by the Court in its 2009 Judgment.

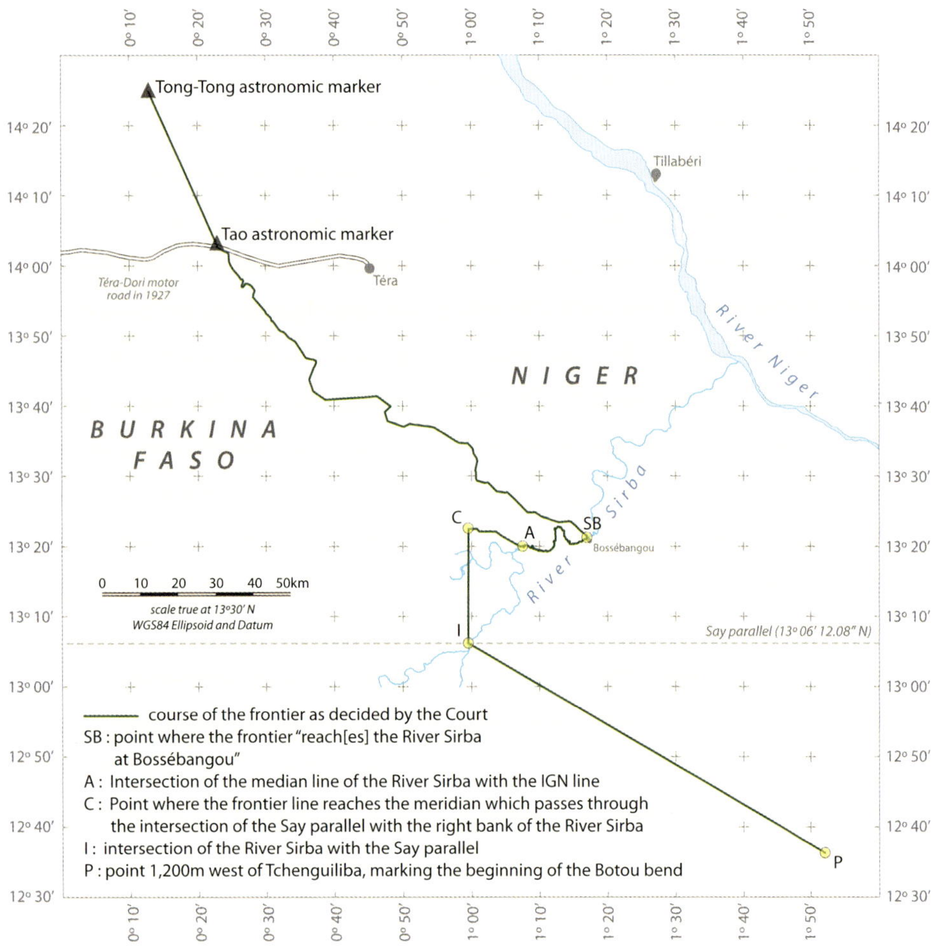

The course of the frontier between Burkina Faso and Niger as decided by the Court in its 2013 Judgment in the Frontier Dispute case.

measures, administrative acts or public works) that could effectively demonstrate a State's display of its sovereign authority over the territory in question.

The Court has been called on to clarify the relationship between "titles" and *effectivités*, particularly in cases involving territories that have gained independence as a result of decolonization. On these occasions, it has enshrined, among others, the principle of the intangibility of boundaries inherited from colonization or *uti possidetis juris* which ensures respect for the territorial boundaries that existed when independence was achieved and for stable neighbourly relations between States.

If the parties so request, after determining which State has sovereignty over the territory in dispute, the Court may be asked to plot the course of the boundary between them, or even assist them in implementing its decision. For example, in the cases concerning *Frontier Dispute*, between Burkina Faso and Mali and Burkina Faso and Niger, respectively, the Court was seised by special agreement asking it to appoint three experts to help the Parties to the proceedings demarcate their shared boundaries in the areas in dispute. In both cases, the Court made an Order appointing the experts in question after delivering its Judgment on the merits.

The delimitation of maritime boundaries

The Court has also played an important role in developing international maritime delimitation law. Disputes in this area began to emerge as States appropriated ever-greater maritime spaces off their coasts in which to explore and exploit natural resources. The law of the sea, which lays down the rules applicable to the delimitation of maritime spaces, is an area of the law that has been largely codified, first by the 1958 Geneva Conventions on the territorial sea, on the high seas, on fishing and conservation of the living resources of the high seas, and on the continental shelf, and then by the 1982 United Nations Convention on the Law of the Sea (UNCLOS).

In determining the course of maritime boundaries in the cases before it, the Court has applied and interpreted both the fundamental concepts of the law of the sea, such as the territorial sea, the continental shelf and the exclusive economic zone (EEZ), maritime areas over which coastal States exercise jurisdiction and hold certain rights, and the principles applicable to the delimitation of such areas. The Court's decisions on these questions complemented, and sometimes inspired, the development of the rules set out in the conventions concluded in this area.

For example, in its 1969 Judgment in the *North Sea Continental Shelf (Denmark/Federal Republic of Germany; Federal Republic of Germany/Netherlands)* cases, in which the Court was asked to determine the principles and rules of international law applicable to the delimitation of the North Sea continental shelf between the parties, the Court established the rule that all maritime delimitations must be effected by agreement between the States concerned, which must be reached in accordance with equitable principles.

This approach influenced the work of the Third United Nations Conference on the Law of the Sea, which codified the rule that the delimitation of the continental shelf and the EEZ should be effected by agreement resulting in an equitable solution. The ICJ's subsequent jurisprudence confirmed the application, in the area of delimitation, of equitable principles and the use of methods aimed at securing an equitable result.

Through its jurisprudence, the Court has gradually clarified and helped harmonize certain rules and methods applicable to the delimitation of various maritime areas. While the law of the sea distinguishes between the delimitation of territorial seas, on the one hand, and the delimitation of the continental shelf and EEZs, on the other, in practice the Court is increasingly called on by States to determine a single maritime boundary delimiting their respective territorial seas, continental shelves and EEZs. In its Judgments in the cases concerning *Maritime Delimitation in the Black Sea (Romania* v. *Ukraine)*, in 2009, and *Territorial and Maritime Dispute (Nicaragua* v. *Colombia)*, in 2012, the Court delimited various maritime spaces using the so-called three-step method, which consists of first drawing a provisional line, on which every point is the same distance away from whatever point is nearest to it on the coast of each of the countries concerned, then examining the circumstances that may justify an adjustment of that line in order to achieve an equitable result and, finally, verifying that the line obtained does not give rise to an inequitable result by comparing the ratio between maritime areas and respective coastal lengths.

While the Court has generally used this three-step method in the cases before it, it has been careful to make clear that this method should not be applied in a mechanical fashion.

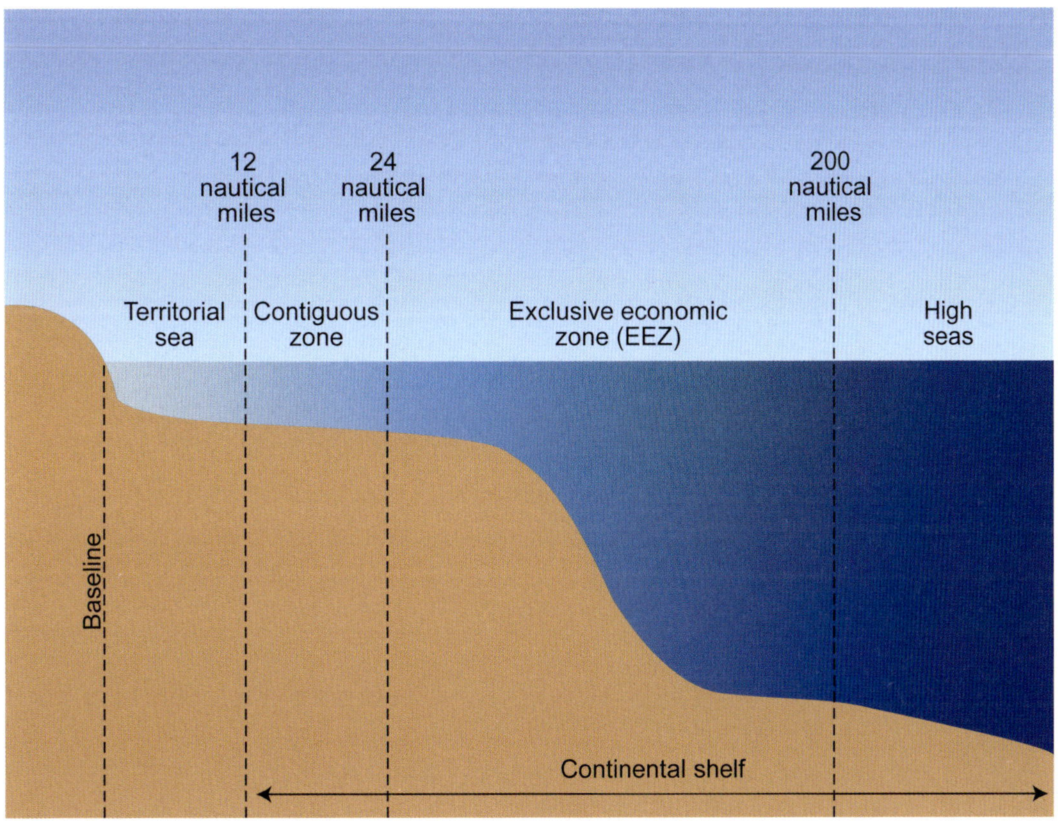

The boundaries of the territorial sea, contiguous zone, exclusive economic zone and continental shelf, as defined in UNCLOS.

It has thus determined that it will not always be appropriate to begin with a provisional equidistance (or median) line, for instance when such a line is not feasible. The three-step method, as established by the Court, has also been used by other international judicial bodies, such as the International Tribunal for the Law of the Sea and a number of arbitral tribunals. The Court's jurisprudence has therefore had a decisive influence on the method used by other competent international courts and tribunals. In their decisions, those institutions now refer to each other, thereby contributing to the coherence of international maritime delimitation law.

Owing to the technical nature of maritime delimitation cases, it may be useful for the Court to appoint experts to assist it in examining the evidence submitted by the parties. For example, in 2016, in the case concerning *Maritime Delimitation in the Caribbean Sea and the Pacific Ocean (Costa Rica* v. *Nicaragua)*, the Court appointed two experts to provide technical expertise in order to ascertain the state of the coast between each of the points presented by the Parties as the starting-point of their maritime boundary in the Caribbean Sea.

The Court's jurisprudence has helped clarify the rules and principles applicable to territorial and maritime delimitation; it has also contributed to the development of a methodology that guarantees stability, predictability and consistency in this area of international law. Moreover, in some cases the Court's decisions have assisted in easing tensions between the parties to a dispute, fostering better neighbourly relations between them. •

The three-step delimitation process as illustrated in the Court's 2018 Judgment in two joined cases between Costa Rica and Nicaragua

1

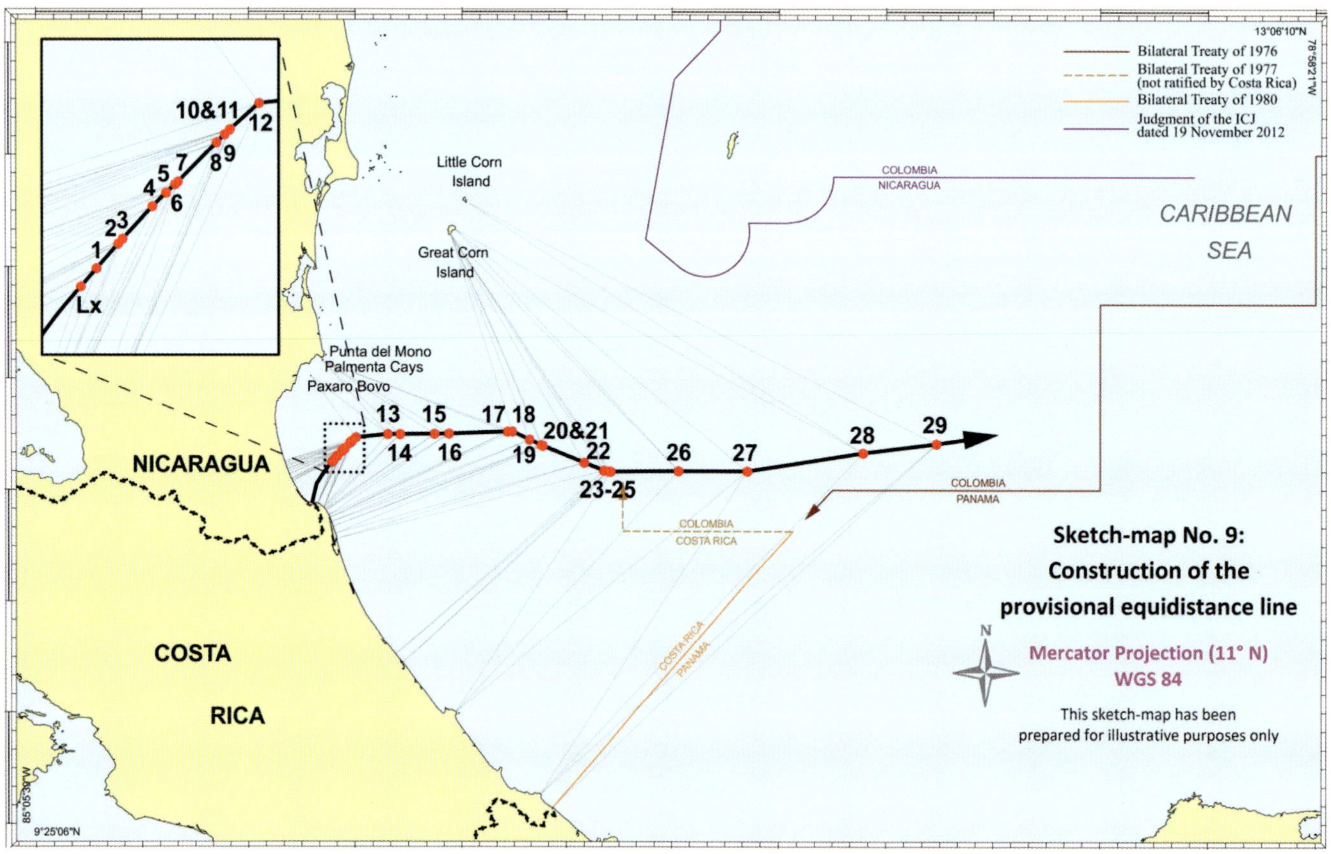

Construction of a provisional line, every point of which is equidistant from the nearest point on the coast of each of the countries concerned.

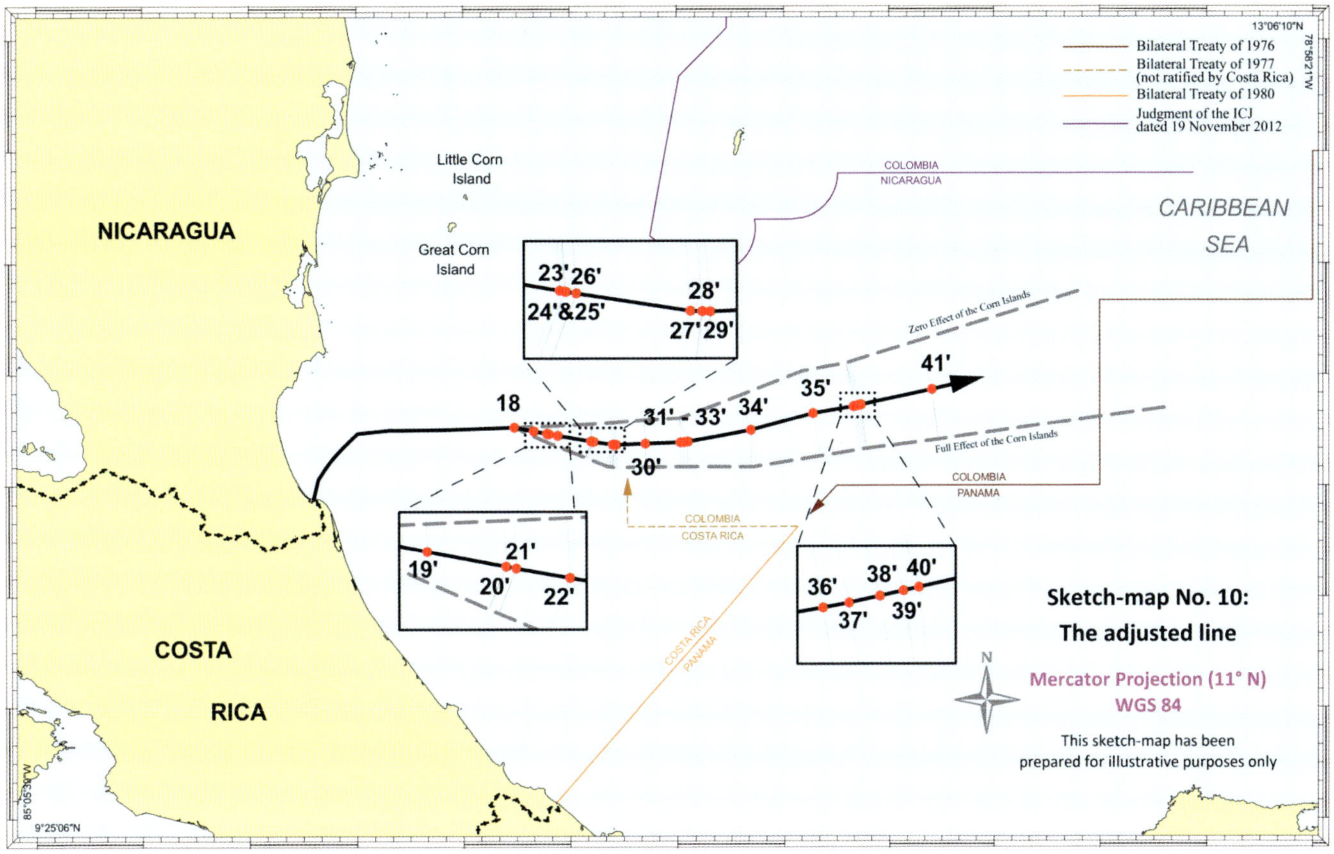

Sketch-map No. 10: The adjusted line

2

Adjustment of the provisional line in order to achieve an equitable result, taking certain circumstances into account.

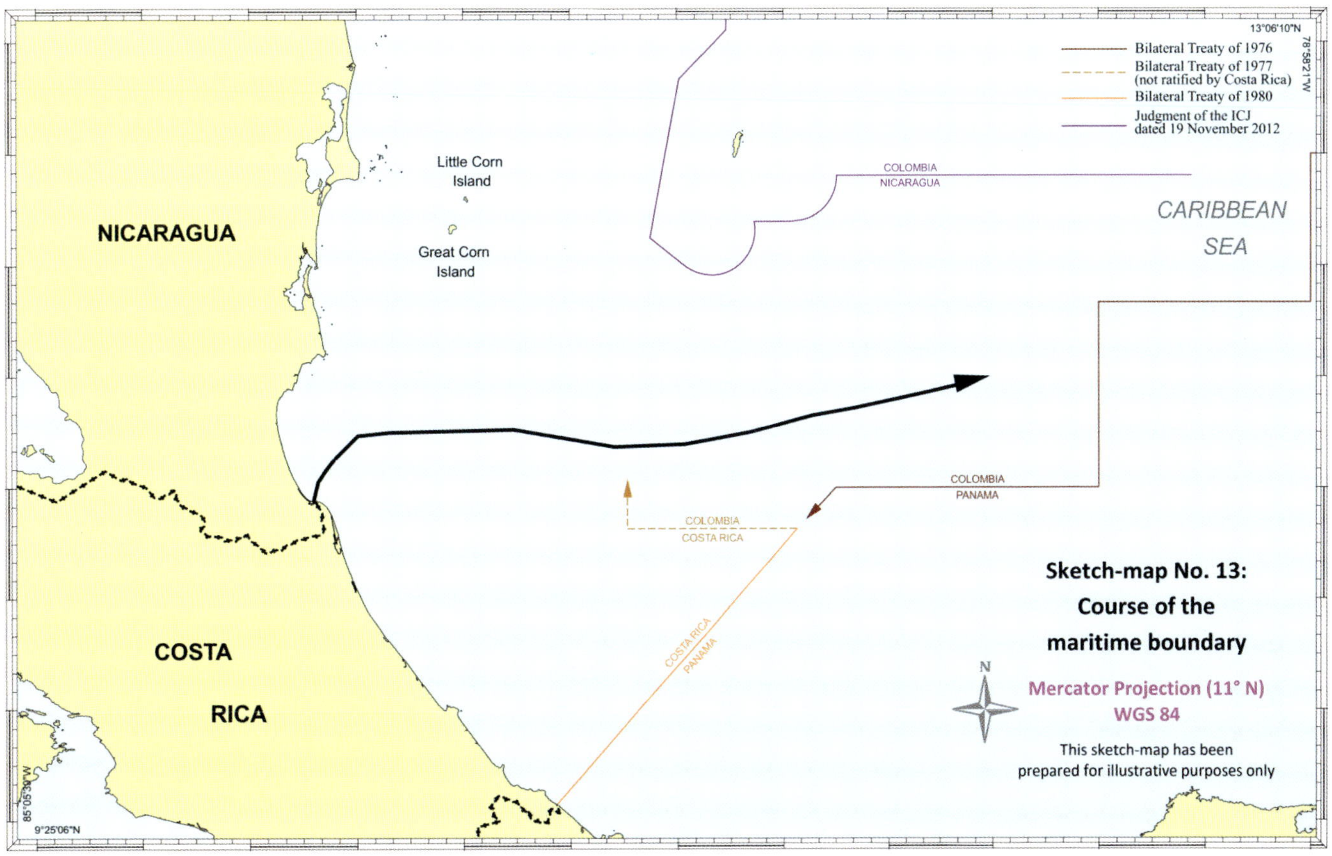

Sketch-map No. 13: Course of the maritime boundary

3

Course of the maritime boundary after verifying that no disproportionality is created between the maritime areas attributed to each Party.

OUTREACH AND TRAINING ACTIVITIES

The Registry of the ICJ produces a wide range of information material for various audiences, from those simply wishing to learn more about the Court and its activities to those planning a career in international law.

Outreach and training activities take several forms, including presentations, tours, educational workshops and conferences, and the Court's internship and Judicial Fellowship programmes. In addition to the ICJ website, the ICJ app, the Court's social media platforms, multimedia material and various publications, the Registry is also responsible for the ICJ Museum, which is housed in the Peace Palace.

The ICJ Museum

In the late 1980s and early 1990s, the number of proceedings before the Court rose substantially. This resulted in a significant growth in media coverage of its activities, which in turn led to a rise in the general awareness of and interest in the Court.

Wishing to foster and enhance the public's understanding of its work, in 1997 the Court began discussing the creation of a permanent exhibition, setting out its history, activities and achievements, as well as those of its predecessor, the Permanent Court of International Justice. The ICJ Museum was opened in May 1999, to coincide with the hundredth anniversary of the First Hague Peace Conference of 1899. Inaugurated by United Nations Secretary-General Kofi Annan, the museum has since welcomed a host of visitors, including students from the Hague Academy of International Law, visiting dignitaries, ambassadors and guests of the Court.

In June 2012, a Visitors' Centre was opened at the entrance to the Peace Palace grounds, allowing an even greater number of visitors to gain an insight into the history of the Palace and the organizations housed therein. To ensure that the ICJ Museum would continue to be used for the educational purposes for which it was first created and to provide detailed information about the Court's jurisdiction, procedure and ongoing activities to those seeking a more complete understanding of its functions, the decision was taken to update and expand its content. Work soon began on the museum's metamorphosis and, in 2016, on the occasion of the seventieth anniversary of the Court, the ICJ Museum was officially opened by United Nations Secretary-General Ban Ki-moon.

The museum's exhibition retraces the major steps in the creation and development of the international judicial institutions housed in the Peace Palace, established to bring about the peaceful settlement of international disputes, focusing in particular on the ICJ. The exhibition showcases material from the Court's archives, such as case-related documents, and includes several items donated by various peace organizations and visiting representatives of States. Information is presented in a range of ways, including audio-visual and electronic formats. In addition, a study area has been created where presentations, workshops and discussions can be hosted by representatives of the Court and its Registry.

Information materials about pending cases before the Court are made available during public sittings.

ICJ outreach activities

The Registry's Information Department, with assistance from the Department of Legal Matters, delivers an average of four to five presentations each week to groups of university students, diplomats, scholars and academics, judges, lawyers, legal professionals and journalists. These presentations offer an in-depth insight into the workings of the Court and often result in enquiries about internships and other career opportunities.

The Information Department also regularly organizes interviews and press conferences, at which questions on the Court's functions and activities may be put to the President or Registrar of the Court.

As part of its outreach activities, the Registry runs workshops introducing younger audiences to the subject of peace and justice and the role of the ICJ. These workshops are typically aimed at 11 and 15 year olds (those close to completing their primary and secondary education, respectively). The Registry of the Court also works closely with the organizers of the Model United Nations programme held annually in The Hague, delivering presentations to large numbers of student delegation members.

Each year, the Registry's Information Department takes part in the Hague International Open Day, marking the annual United Nations International Day of Peace celebrated on 21 September. For one Sunday only, the Court, along with other international organizations based in The Hague, opens its doors to the public, welcoming up to 300 visitors, who get a rare glimpse of the main rooms used by the Court, such as the Great Hall of Justice (the ICJ's courtroom) and the rooms adjacent to it, where the judges meet prior to and during public sittings of the Court. During their tour, visitors also receive a general presentation on the Court and its work from a member of the Information Department, followed by a short question and answer session.

Internships at the Court

The ICJ offers internships of between one and three months to students and young professionals in the early stages of their career. The internship is an opportunity for them to put their knowledge and experience into practice under the supervision of one or more Registry officials. Given the Registry's small size, only a limited number of internships can be offered throughout the year. Internship vacancies are publicized on the ICJ website and through the Court's eRecruitment system.

Judicial Fellowship Programme

The ICJ's Judicial Fellowship Programme, formerly known as the University Traineeship Programme, was established to enable recent law graduates to gain experience working at the ICJ. It aims to improve participants' understanding of international law and of the Court's procedures by actively involving them in the work of the Court and allowing them to build on their experience under the supervision of a judge. The Programme started in 1999, when the Court agreed to allow five graduates from the New York University School of Law to serve as university trainees at the Court. Over the years, the Court has sought to expand the Programme, with a view to increasing the geographical distribution and number of participating universities. Since the Programme was first created, over 200 graduates from more than 35 universities have been given the opportunity to work at the Court, going on to pursue careers in international law as academics, in private practice, or in national or international civil service.

Judicial Fellows are selected from a pool of candidates nominated by universities, who usually have excellent academic results and

The Judicial Fellowship Programme offers graduates the opportunity to work at the ICJ for a period of 10 months.

The Judicial Fellowship Programme opened a door for me to learn directly from the judges and jurists of the Court. I was humbled by peers from all over the world, who possess the same passion (if not more) for international law. The inspiration, encouragement and camaraderie that I received shall be cherished forever.

Bin Jiang, Judicial Fellow 2015-2016

The Judicial Fellowship was one of my first professional experiences and a dream come true for someone wanting to work in international law! I learned a lot from my judge, my colleagues and the other fellows. From speech drafting to legal research on pending cases, I truly believe that the Fellowship gave me the right tools to start my career in this field.

Jessica Joly-Hébert, Judicial Fellow 2015-2016

The chance to observe and learn different perspectives of international law and adjudication from the judges, the opportunity to experience the inner workings of the Court, and being surrounded by a brilliant community of international lawyers all converge to make the Judicial Fellowship Programme a once-in-a-lifetime opportunity. It is undoubtedly the most rewarding experience for any young international lawyer.

Aditya Laddha, Judicial Fellow 2020-2021

have demonstrated an interest in international law through their studies, work or publications. The nominating university funds the stipend, health insurance and travel costs of the Judicial Fellow, if selected. Every year, the Court accepts up to 15 Judicial Fellows, each from a different nominating university, who are each assigned to a Member of the Court for a period of ten months, from September to June or July of the following year. During their fellowship, the Judicial Fellows have the opportunity to conduct research, to write memoranda on legal and factual issues arising in ongoing cases, to attend public hearings of the Court and to work alongside an associate legal officer assigned to the judge.

In recent years, the Court has recognized that financial constraints have prevented many less well-endowed universities, particularly those in developing countries, from nominating candidates for the Judicial Fellowship Programme. To address this, in 2019, the Court proposed the establishment of a trust fund, with a view to improving the Programme's geographic and linguistic diversity and promoting the study and practice of international law.

On 14 December 2020, the United Nations General Assembly adopted resolution 75/129, requesting the Secretary-General to establish and administer a trust fund for the ICJ Judicial Fellowship Programme, to be used to grant fellowship awards to nationals of developing countries from universities based in developing countries, chosen by the Court for the Judicial Fellowship Programme. The award is intended to cover living expenses in The Hague, as well as travel and health insurance costs for the duration of the fellowship. Contributions to the trust fund can be

SVPREMVM

made by States, international financial institutions, donor agencies, intergovernmental and non-governmental organizations, national and private institutions, and bar associations, among others. The trust fund was formally established in the spring of 2021, and it is hoped that it will facilitate access to the Judicial Fellowship Programme for talented young law graduates from all regions of the world.

The Court's website, app and multimedia material

The Court's website is regularly updated to reflect judicial developments in cases pending before it. It provides access to a large collection of resources about the Court and its predecessor, the PCIJ, including a list of all cases heard by the Court, dating back to the first case in 1947, the schedule of upcoming public sittings, relevant legal texts, press releases, case-related filings, video and photographic material, and various publications. The Court's free "CIJ-ICJ" mobile device app enables users to keep abreast of the latest developments at the ICJ, including information on pending and past cases, decisions, press releases and updates to the Court's judicial calendar. It also allows users to receive real-time notifications as soon as decisions or press releases are issued.

In 2021, on the occasion of its seventy-fifth anniversary, the Court launched a new institutional film, which offers an insight into the Court's mission by explaining its role, composition and functioning, and highlighting its contribution to the peaceful resolution of international legal disputes. The Court also launched a virtual tour of the ICJ, which guides viewers through the rooms of the Peace Palace used by the judges when performing their judicial functions. Both the film and virtual tour are available on the Court's website at www.icj-cij.org/en/multimedia-index.

A group visiting the Peace Palace.

ICJ publications

The publications of the ICJ, some of which are available in electronic format, are published by the Registry. They include:

- *Reports of Judgments, Advisory Opinions and Orders:* This series contains both the English and French versions of the Court's decisions. The collected decisions for each year, with an index, are bound in one or several volumes.

- *Pleadings, Oral arguments, Documents:* Volumes in this series are published after the termination of each case and contain the documentation relating to the case in the original language, i.e. English or French. This includes the document instituting proceedings, the written pleadings, the verbatim records of the oral proceedings and any documents submitted to the Court after the closure of the written proceedings.

- *Acts and Documents:* This series contains the UN Charter, the Statute and Rules of Court, along with Practice Directions and other basic texts.

- *Annuaire-Yearbook:* Each year a *Yearbook* is published describing the work of the Court from 1 August of the preceding year to 31 July of the current year. This publication used to be issued in separate English *(Yearbook)* and French *(Annuaire)* versions. Since No. 68, it has been published as a bilingual version.

- *Bibliography:* The Registry regularly issues a bibliography listing the works and documents referring to the Court that have come to its attention during the previous year.

- *Handbook:* The *Handbook* aims to provide the general public with a simple, comprehensible overview of the history, composition, jurisdiction, procedure and decisions of the Court.

Useful links

- You can find out about upcoming public proceedings through the calendar of events and hearings available on the ICJ website at www.icj-cij.org/en/calendar. Proceedings and events are usually announced between one and three weeks in advance.

- To receive ICJ press releases, fill out the form on the following page of the website: www.icj-cij.org/en/mailing-list

- The Court's interactive toolkit is a great source of basic information about the ICJ's history, role and functioning, and is available to download at www.icj-cij.org/en/basic-toolkit

- Proceedings of the Court are broadcast live and in full on the ICJ website. You are advised to check the feed 10 minutes prior to the start of a particular sitting on the ICJ homepage: www.icj-cij.org

- You can find out more about the Court's Judicial Fellowship Programme at www.icj-cij.org/en/judicial-fellows-program

- For information on how to apply to attend a presentation or workshop, go to the following page of the Court's website: www.icj-cij.org/en/presentations-work-of-the-court

- The ICJ recruits staff in both the Professional (P) and General Service (GS) categories. Vacancy announcements can be found at www.icj-cij.org/en/current-vacancies or on the Court's LinkedIn page.

- The Court's regular publications, including *Reports of Judgments, Advisory Opinions and Orders*, *Pleadings, Oral Arguments, Documents*, the Court's *Annuaire-Yearbook*, the *Handbook* and the *Bibliography*, can be purchased from the Sales and Marketing Section of the United Nations Secretariat at: United Nations Publications, 405 East 42nd Street, Room S-09FW001, New York, NY 10017, United States of America.
  Email: publications@un.org
  Website: shop.un.org

The Yearbook describes the work of the Court over one year, from 1 August to 31 July.

The Court's Twitter account, YouTube channel and LinkedIn page are all extremely useful tools at your disposal:

- **ICJ Twitter account:** @CIJ_ICJ
- **YouTube channel:** CIJ_ICJ
- **LinkedIn page:** International Court of Justice (ICJ)

COUR
DE JUSTICE
INTERNATIONAL
OF

CONCLUSION: POSSIBLE CHALLENGES FOR THE COURT IN THE FUTURE

Seventy-five years after the adoption of the Charter of the United Nations, the Court remains an essential tool of global governance thanks to its quantitative and qualitative contribution to the development of the international rule of law and the peaceful settlement of disputes. The Court has been seised of more contentious cases in the last 25 years than it was during the first 50 years of its existence. Entire fields of international law are either based on its jurisprudence or have been clarified by its judgments.

To remain ever relevant in the years ahead, the Court will need to overcome present and future challenges. One of the challenges it faces at present, and which may well extend into the future, arises from the unintended consequences of the Court's success, namely the heavy workload that the growing number of cases has placed on the Court's support services. Another challenge on which the Court's future success also depends is whether States will continue to be willing to settle their disputes peacefully through recourse to the Court. A third challenge may arise from emerging global threats, such as environmental degradation, global warming and pandemics, to name but a few, which may require new approaches to the interpretation and application of international law and to the judicial settlement of complex international disputes.

The Court's increased workload and the consequences for its support services

The growing number of cases submitted to the Court is a positive development that shows that States increasingly trust the Court to help settle their disputes in an impartial and efficient manner. This increased number of cases translates into a heavier workload not only for Members of the Court, but especially for the Court's support services. Although often hidden from the general public, services such as the Department of Legal Matters, the Department of Linguistic Matters and the Text Processing and Reproduction Division are a critical link in the chain, ensuring the quality of the Court's judicial decisions and its overall efficiency. Yet they have relatively few staff members, who have to deal with the Court handling several cases simultaneously and the very tight deadlines set by the Court for the production of its judgments.

In addition, the COVID-19 pandemic has had a serious impact on the Court's budgetary and staffing requirements. The shift to hybrid and remote public sittings and deliberations has resulted in significant costs in terms of new technological tools and qualified staff capable of handling them. Mindful of the overall budgetary situation of the United Nations, however, the Court has always remained very conservative in its budgetary requests to the General Assembly. The budget of the Court is around US$30 million, less than 1 per cent of the budget of the United Nations, of which it is the principal judicial organ. It is one of the smallest annual budgets ever allocated to a court or a tribunal established by the United Nations or under its auspices. The Registry of the Court is composed of just 117 staff members, a number that has not increased significantly in the last two decades. It is therefore clear that, if the number of cases submitted to the Court continues to increase, the Court will need a budget and staff commensurate with its responsibilities and reflecting its critical importance in the peaceful settlement of disputes.

Members of the Court take their seats at the Bench.

How the means of accepting the Court's jurisdiction have evolved

The way in which disputes are brought to the Court is of vital importance to the success of its work. When the Statute of the Permanent Court of International Justice, the Court's predecessor, was drafted in 1920, it was thought that the system of optional clause declarations under Article 36, paragraph 2, of the Statute would be the best means by which disputes could be brought before the Court. This turned out not to be so, however. Rather, the majority of cases brought before the Court have been founded on compromissory clauses in bilateral or multilateral treaties: over the last 75 years, 61 cases have been submitted to the Court solely on the basis of compromissory clauses, including 44 cases based on multilateral treaties. In comparison, only 27 cases have been submitted to the Court during this period based solely on optional declarations under Article 36, paragraph 2, of the Statute. Of the 15 cases pending before the Court as of 1 November 2021, at least nine call for the interpretation and application of a multilateral treaty.

However, the practice of including compromissory clauses in multilateral and bilateral treaties appears to be decreasing. Multilateral conventions are less common today and, very often, even those that are concluded under the auspices of the United Nations do not include a compromissory clause referring to the Court as a means of dispute settlement. This might constitute a challenge to the Court in the future: if this trend continues, it may gradually reduce the scope of the Court's jurisdiction and lead to a substantial reduction in the number of cases brought before it.

It is unlikely that the need for States to consent to the jurisdiction of the Court will change in the foreseeable future, but the means by which such consent is expressed might continue to evolve. It therefore falls to the Court and other principal organs of the United Nations, such as the General Assembly and the Security Council, to give some thought to this development and, where necessary, come up with new ideas and suggestions for alternative means of securing the consent of States to the jurisdiction of the Court or for strengthening the means already in existence.

List of cases currently pending before the Court (order by date of introduction)

1. *Gabčíkovo-Nagymaros Project (Hungary/Slovakia)*
2. *Armed Activities on the Territory of the Congo (Democratic Republic of the Congo v. Uganda)*
3. *Question of the Delimitation of the Continental Shelf between Nicaragua and Colombia beyond 200 Nautical Miles from the Nicaraguan Coast (Nicaragua v. Colombia)*
4. *Alleged Violations of Sovereign Rights and Maritime Spaces in the Caribbean Sea (Nicaragua v. Colombia)*
5. *Dispute over the Status and Use of the Waters of the Silala (Chile v. Bolivia)*
6. *Certain Iranian Assets (Islamic Republic of Iran v. United States of America)*
7. *Application of the International Convention for the Suppression of the Financing of Terrorism and of the International Convention on the Elimination of All Forms of Racial Discrimination (Ukraine v. Russian Federation)*
8. *Arbitral Award of 3 October 1899 (Guyana v. Venezuela)*
9. *Alleged Violations of the 1955 Treaty of Amity, Economic Relations, and Consular Rights (Islamic Republic of Iran v. United States of America)*
10. *Relocation of the United States Embassy to Jerusalem (Palestine v. United States of America)*
11. *Guatemala's Territorial, Insular and Maritime Claim (Guatemala/Belize)*
12. *Application of the Convention on the Prevention and Punishment of the Crime of Genocide (The Gambia v. Myanmar)*
13. *Land and Maritime Delimitation and Sovereignty over Islands (Gabon/Equatorial Guinea)*
14. *Application of the International Convention on the Elimination of All Forms of Racial Discrimination (Armenia v. Azerbaijan)*
15. *Application of the International Convention on the Elimination of All Forms of Racial Discrimination (Azerbaijan v. Armenia)*

The role of the Court in new challenges faced by humanity

The Court must also be mindful of the legal issues and disputes that may arise in the future from new challenges faced by humanity, such as global warming, environmental degradation, cyber threats and other emerging issues associated with the use of new technology. These are all questions that often transcend national frontiers and may give rise to multifaceted and multilateral disputes that require new legal approaches and responses for them to be settled peacefully.

It is still not clear, however, whether these issues will be regulated by States through multilateral treaty frameworks or through soft-law instruments and institutional diplomacy, or whether States will entrust the Court with the task of settling potential disputes in these areas. It is also unclear whether, in the absence of multilateral instruments regulating such global issues, States will approach the Court and request it to play its classic role of judicial settlement of disputes by giving appropriate responses on the basis of existing principles and rules of international law. The answer to this question will determine the extent to which the Court will be able to contribute to developments in new areas of international law through its dispute settlement function.

To take the example of global warming, it is well known that in some European countries domestic courts have already been called upon to determine the compliance of their governments with the commitments they have made in such international instruments as the 2015 Paris Agreement on Climate Change and the United Nations Framework Convention on Climate Change (UNFCC). These cases concern measures that must be adopted domestically to reduce emissions or move towards a low-carbon economy. However, disputes between States could arise as a result of the action or inaction of a State on global warming that affects other States and their populations.

The Court will therefore have to stay attuned to the evolving needs of the global community in this field, since it might be called upon to deal with such disputes and the associated complex factual and scientific issues. While the Court's Statute provides the necessary flexibility for the Court to process large-scale litigation and complex scientific matters, it will nevertheless be a challenge for the Court to adjudicate in a field where the law is lagging far behind fast-paced developments in the state of the global environment. Having had to confront similar challenges in the past, however, there is no doubt that the Court will be able to deal with new ones and harness the rules and principles of international law to find peaceful solutions to thorny disputes between States.

Judge Abdulqawi Ahmed Yusuf
Member of the Court

Photography credits

Photograph sources are indicated below in alphabetical order:

Photographic collection of the ICJ: ©UN Photo/ICJ-CIJ

Pages 19 (above left, above right, below left), 35 (above). Frank van Beek: cover page and pages 2, 8, 20, 25 (right), 28, 32, 36, 43, 48, 50, 52, 55, 59, 61, 62, 65 (above left, below left and right), 68-69, 75, 81 (below), 85 (above left, middle left and right, below left), 86, 94, 100, 104-105, 106, 108, 111. Frank van Beek: Frank van Beek/ANP-in-Opdracht: pages 70, 82. Frank van Beek and Rob Ris, Max Koot Studios: Page 30. Wendy van Bree: Page 7. Broad Red Media: Page 65 (above right). Jeroen Bouman: Pages 56, 81 (above). Gerald van Daalen: Pages 35 (below), 73. Nils van Houts: Page 33. Bastiaan van Musscher: Page 40 (below right). Rob Ris, Max Koot Studios: Pages 11, 40 (above right). Hadewych Veys: Page 88.

Other photos

Lybil Ber ©Lybil Ber: Pages 10, 12, 23, 25 (left), 26-27, 39, 67, 85 (above right, below right), 102. Carnegie Foundation Peace Palace ©Carnegie Foundation/Peace Palace: Pages 6-7, 22, 24. Imperial War Museum Collection: IWM A31242: Page 19. Peter van der Plas ©Peter van der Plas, PE-Fotostudio: Page 40 (above left). United Nations Photo Library: ©UN Photo: Pages 16-17, 31 (Evan Schneider, left; Eskinder Debebe, right), 40 (Mark Garten, below left), 44 (Yutaka Nagata), 76 (Eskinder Debebe).

Case-related material

Page 73, sketch-map, *Request for Interpretation of the Judgment of 15 June 1962 in the Case concerning the* Temple of Preah Vihear (Cambodia *v.* Thailand) *(Cambodia* v. *Thailand), Provisional Measures, Order of 18 July 2011, I.C.J. Reports 2011 (II)*, p. 553. Page 91, *Gabčíkovo-Nagymaros Project (Hungary/Slovakia)*, Memorial of Hungary, Annexes, Vol. 2, 2 May 1994, Map No. 3. Page 92, Memorial of Costa Rica on Compensation, *Certain Activities Carried Out by Nicaragua in the Border Area (Costa Rica* v. *Nicaragua)* and *Construction of a Road in Costa Rica along the San Juan River (Nicaragua* v. *Costa Rica)*, p. 30, Figure 3.4. Page 96, *Frontier Dispute (Burkina Faso/Niger), Judgment, I.C.J. Reports 2013*, p. 91, sketch-map No. 4. Page 97, Graphic, ICJ-CIJ. Pages 98-99, *Maritime Delimitation in the Caribbean Sea and the Pacific Ocean (Costa Rica* v. *Nicaragua)* and *Land Boundary in the Northern Part of Isla Portillos (Costa Rica* v. *Nicaragua), Judgment, I.C.J. Reports 2018 (I)*, pp. 194, 199, 204, sketch-maps Nos. 9, 10, 13.

COUR INTERNATIONALE DE JUSTICE

INTERNATIONAL COURT OF JUSTICE